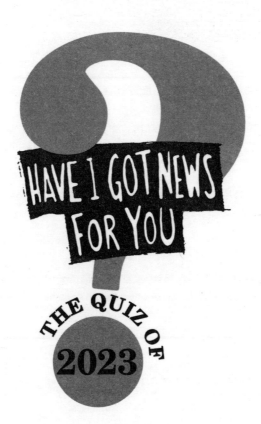

HAVE I GOT NEWS FOR YOU

THE QUIZ OF 2023

WRITTEN BY DAN BOWMAN

SPHERE

SPHERE

First published in Great Britain in 2023 by Sphere

1 3 5 7 9 10 8 6 4 2

Copyright © Hat Trick Productions Ltd 2023
Written by Dan Bowman

The moral right of the author has been asserted.

A CIP catalogue record for this book
is available from the British Library.

ISBN 978-1-4087-2711-9

Typeset in Plantin by M Rules
Printed and bound in Great Britain by
Clays Ltd, Elcograf S.p.A.

Papers used by Sphere are from well-managed forests
and other responsible sources.

Sphere
An imprint of
Little, Brown Book Group
Carmelite House
50 Victoria Embankment
London EC4Y 0DZ

An Hachette UK Company
www.hachette.co.uk

www.littlebrown.co.uk

Introduction

After the Brexity-Covid years of 2020 and 2021, and the Ukraine/cost-of-living crisis/prime-minister-turnover implosion of 2022, at first glance you'd be forgiven for thinking 2023 wasn't quite so jam-packed. But don't be fooled – whether it was Harry over-sharing about his todger in his autobiography, or celebrities from Gary Lineker to Phillip Schofield to Huw Edwards to Russell Brand dominating the news agenda, plus strikes, inflation, wildfires, the Wagner group mounting the briefest mutiny of all time, an ill-fated trip to the *Titanic* and – as usual – a stack of scandals leaking out of the cabinet, 2023 has had just as many events you'd like to forget as any other year. Before you can do that though, we're going to quiz you on them.

This book is packed full of rounds that will hopefully make reflecting on another chaotic year a little bit more fun. There's the missing words round, odd one out, ~~stolen~~ borrowed formats from other quizzes, wordsearches, crosswords, mazes and – as a word of warning – some close-up photographs of Michael Fabricant.

It's also worth mentioning that just as last year's book went to print, there were two major deaths (the Queen, and Liz Truss's political career) so if anyone mentioned in this one has selfishly kicked the bucket, or if there's been a general election and Keir Starmer is commanding a cabinet of people you've never heard of inside No. 10, that's why it's not referenced. Printing and distributing a book takes about the same amount of time as exporting a lorry full of mackerel to the EU, and as such we went to print in the second week of January. (Just kidding, it was mid-September.)

So sit back, try not to worry about where your next mortgage payment is coming from, and enjoy *Have I Got News for You: The Quiz of 2023.*

WHO AM I?

The statements below all relate to people who featured in the news in 2023. Can you match them up?

1. In April I became the first person to make a maximum break in the final of the World Snooker Championship, although despite this I still lost.
2. I performed at the 2023 Super Bowl half-time show while pregnant with my second child.
3. I am a British criminal who shares a name with an American actor. I have been behind bars since 1974 and in March I was refused parole.
4. I am a British fashion supremo who was named a Companion of Honour in King Charles's birthday honours in June, having already received a damehood in 2017.
5. I am the smooth-headed chancellor of Germany. My government finally agreed to send tanks to Ukraine in March after months of shuffling its feet.
6. I am a British comedian with a successful late-night show on Channel 4. I also hosted the 2023 BRIT Awards.
7. I am a veteran Italian jockey who announced my plans to retire at the end of the 2023 season. In June I achieved my eightieth and eighty-first wins at Royal Ascot.
8. I am an Irish actor, with credits including *Peaky Blinders* and *28 Days Later*. In 2023 I took on the lead role in Christopher Nolan's *Oppenheimer*.

9. I'm a British artist who once plonked a bed in the middle of the Tate Gallery. When the National Portrait Gallery was revamped for 2023 I was commissioned to create the doors.

10. I'm the lead singer of the Bangles, and in 2023 I released my first novel, *This Bird Has Flown*, to widespread acclaim.

11. I played my last ever UK show in June, and completed the highest-grossing stadium tour of all time three weeks later. I'm not particularly fond of the paparazzi.

12. I'm an Italian TV chef and panel-show regular who travelled around the world with Gordon Ramsay and Fred Sirieix until March 2023, when I left them to their own devices.

13. I'm a television personality who received praise in 2023 for a groundbreaking documentary about the effects of female contraception, which aired on Channel 4 in June.

14. I'm a former rugby player who takes on increasingly difficult challenges for charity. In May I carried a close friend across the finish line of the Leeds Marathon.

15. I am the prime minister of Italy, described by some as the country's most right-wing leader since Mussolini.

16. I'm an American politician who celebrated my one hundredth birthday in May. I served as secretary of state under Richard Nixon and Gerald Ford. I received the Nobel Peace Prize in 1973, but there are a lot of people who think it was undeserved.

17. I'm a British Canadian tennis player who won the US Open in 2021 and have since struggled with injuries. In 2023 I underwent surgery on my ankle and both wrists.

18. I'm a ginger-haired rock frontman who enjoyed great success in the late 1980s but then disappeared from public life for much of the 1990s. My band toured the UK in 2023, including a headline appearance at Glastonbury.

19. I'm a Mexican American film actress whose credits include *Frida*, *Desperado* and *From Dusk till Dawn*. In 2023 I played myself in an episode of *Black Mirror*.

20. I'm a humanitarian and author who spent four years as a hostage in the Middle East from 1987 to 1991. In June I was knighted by King Charles.

A. Cillian Murphy	K. Anna Wintour
B. Davina McCall	L. Olaf Scholz
C. Kevin Sinfield	M. Gino D'Acampo
D. Susanna Hoffs	N. Rihanna
E. Elton John	O. Charles Bronson
F. Axl Rose	P. Giorgia Meloni
G. Henry Kissinger	Q. Mark Selby
H. Salma Hayek	R. Emma Raducanu
I. Terry Waite	S. Mo Gilligan
J. Frankie Dettori	T. Tracey Emin

Who Am I? – Answers

1. Q – Mark Selby
2. N – Rihanna
3. O – Charles Bronson
4. K – Anna Wintour
5. L – Olaf Scholz
6. S – Mo Gilligan
7. J – Frankie Dettori
8. A – Cillian Murphy
9. T – Tracey Emin
10. D – Susanna Hoffs

11. E – Elton John
12. M – Gino D'Acampo
13. B – Davina McCall
14. C – Kevin Sinfield
15. P – Giorgia Meloni
16. G – Henry Kissinger
17. R – Emma Raducanu
18. F – Axl Rose
19. H – Salma Hayek
20. I – Terry Waite

Boris Johnson's Last Stand

On 7 December 2021, ITV News released a video of Downing Street Press Secretary Allegra Stratton joking about a Christmas gathering that took place at No. 10, setting in motion a chain of events which would play a huge part in Boris Johnson not only being ousted as prime minister in 2022, but also resigning as an MP in 2023. Here are ten questions about the long-awaited Privileges Committee Report, and the predictably messy fallout.

1. After receiving an initial draft of the report, Boris Johnson immediately resigned as an MP, which must have come as devastating news to his constituents in . . .

    A. Tottenham
    B. Greenwich and Woolwich
    C. Battersea
    D. Uxbridge and South Ruislip

2. When the Privileges Committee report was made public on 15 June, it became apparent why Boris Johnson was rattled. As well as recommending a ninety-day suspension (which could have triggered a recall petition and possible by-election had he not already stepped down), the report also stated that he should be stripped of what?

    A. His parliamentary pass

    B. The allowance awarded to former prime ministers

    C. His taxpayer-funded security team

    D. His citizenship

3. In response to the report, Boris Johnson released a 1,678-word statement/rant, which was especially critical of which Labour MP, who had acted as chair of the committee?

    A. Emily Thornberry

    B. Harriet Harman

    C. Lisa Nandy

    D. Dawn Butler

4. One day after the report was published, the *Daily Mail* announced Boris Johnson as its new columnist, but – because old habits die hard – he was immediately accused of a rule breach by the Advisory Committee on Business Appointments. Why?

    A. He refused to disclose his salary

    B. He'd exceeded the number of jobs a former MP can apply for

    C. He didn't notify them

    D. He did notify them, but only thirty minutes before the announcement

5. Which important issue did Boris Johnson tackle in his first column for the *Daily Mail*?

    A. Slimming pills

    B. E-scooters

    C. Birdwatching

    D. Peat-free compost

6. Two weeks after the release of the main report, a follow-up investigation accused ten people – including Andrea Jenkyns, Michael Fabricant and Brendan Clarke-Smith – of doing what?

    A. Attending lockdown parties

    B. Interfering with the partygate probe

    C. Breaching the MP code of conduct

    D. Trying to block the release of the initial report

7. Which minister resigned following the release of the second report, piling pressure on Rishi Sunak in the process?

    A. Zac Goldsmith
    B. Grant Shapps
    C. Penny Mordaunt
    D. Gillian Keegan

8. A week on from the second Privileges Committee report, Rishi Sunak said that he hadn't read it 'cover to cover'. Why were eyebrows raised at this claim?

    A. He previously said that he'd already read the entire report
    B. There weren't any hard copies
    C. No. 10 claimed he'd missed PMQs in order to 'digest the report'
    D. The entire report was only three pages long

9. Partygate would continue to cause headaches for Rishi Sunak even after Boris Johnson resigned. In July, police confirmed that they were to investigate another lockdown party which took place at Conservative HQ on 8 December 2020. What – according to the invite – was the party called?

    A. Drinks and High Jinks
    B. Jingle and Mingle
    C. Hands, Face, Bass
    D. Black Out to Help Out

10. The contest triggered in Boris Johnson's constituency provided a rare by-election win for the Conservatives. What did Labour blame for the loss?

    A. People staying at home due to bad weather

    B. Voter ID laws

    C. London's Ultra Low Emission Zone

    D. Jeremy Corbyn

Boris Johnson's Last Stand – Answers

1. D – Boris Johnson resigned as the MP for Uxbridge and South Ruislip, which he once briefly visited after taking the wrong exit on the M25.

2. A – The report recommended that Boris Johnson should be stripped of his parliamentary pass, which is traditionally given to ex-MPs to ensure that when the lobbying work dries up they can still buy a subsidised omelette.

3. B – Labour's Harriet Harman acted as chair (although the committee had an overall Tory majority). Johnson's statement also lashed out at Sir Bernard Jenkin due to reports that he'd also hosted a party during lockdown, although it's possible he was just angry that he hadn't been invited.

4. D – Boris Johnson only notified ACOBA (the Advisory Committee on Business Appointments) thirty minutes before the announcement of his new column. ACOBA requires sufficient time to advise on jobs for former MPs and they're still trying to clear the backlog caused by George Osborne in 2017.

5. A – Of all the issues facing the world in 2023, Boris Johnson used his new column to discuss his use of slimming pills to combat '11.30 p.m. fridge raids for cheddar and chorizo'. Some commentators described him as a pound-shop Adrian Chiles, which is just an unnecessarily long-winded way of saying Adrian Chiles.

6. B – The report accused Andrea Jenkyns, Michael Fabricant, Brendan Clarke-Smith and others of interfering

with the Privileges Committee report. It was especially critical of Jacob Rees-Mogg and Nadine Dorries for using their shows on TalkTV and GB News to mount their attacks, which would have amplified their message to at least twenty people.

7. A – Zac Goldsmith resigned as Minister for the International Environment and launched a scathing attack on the PM for perceived apathy on green issues. It must have been a confusing twenty-four hours for Rishi Sunak, as goldsmith is usually the bloke he commissions to make his cutlery.

8. D – Eyebrows were raised at Rishi Sunak's claim that he hadn't read the report 'cover to cover' as the whole thing was only three pages long. He did finally agree to read it, however, and took a private jet to the nearest hard copy.

9. B – Invites for the party at Conservative HQ revealed that it was called 'Jingle and Mingle'. It was attended by failed London mayoral candidate Shaun Bailey, who – in true Tory fashion – was punished with a peerage.

10. C – Labour blamed Sadiq Khan's proposed expansion of the Ultra Low Emission Zone. Ironically, Labour lost by 495 votes, and 893 people voted for the Green Party, therefore handing the win to a party opposed to tackling emissions. Despite the narrow win, the by-election did offer a glimpse of hope for the Tories, who could win the next general election if London's ULEZ is rolled out across the whole of the UK.

Liz Truss, We Hardly Knew Ye (Bonus Round)

When last year's *Have I Got News for You* book went to print, Liz Truss had just become PM. When writing began on this one, Liz Truss was no longer PM. She's not getting off that easily though, so can you work out whether the following things were longer or shorter than her forty-nine-day reign?

1. David Blaine's 2003 'Above the Below' stunt, in which he was suspended over the River Thames in a Perspex box with no access to food.

2. Bryan Adams's stint at number one in the UK Singles Chart with 1991 hit '(Everything I Do) I Do It for You'.

3. The longest ever continuous flight, achieved by a Cessna 172 in 1959.

4. William Henry Harrison's time in office as the ninth president of the United States.

5. The Anglo-Zanzibar War of 1896.

6. Hulk Hogan's first WWE (then WWF) title reign after defeating The Iron Sheik at Madison Square Garden on 23 January 1984.

7. The construction of Mini Sky City, a fifty-seven-storey Chinese skyscraper that was completed in 2015.

8. Nuno Espírito Santo's run as Tottenham manager after replacing José Mourinho in 2021.

9. Activist (and former *Have I Got News for You* panellist) Dan 'Swampy' Hooper's time spent in tunnels beneath the A30 in Devon, before being removed by police in 1996.

10. The 2022 Conservative leadership contest, which she won to become PM in the first place.

Liz Truss, We Hardly Knew Ye (Bonus Round) – Answers

Longer than Liz Truss's reign as PM

2. Bryan Adams's stint at number one in the UK Singles Chart with 1991 hit '(Everything I Do) I Do It for You' – **112 days**

3. The longest ever continuous flight, achieved by a Cessna 172 in 1959 – **64 days**

6. Hulk Hogan's first WWE (then WWF) title reign after defeating The Iron Sheik at Madison Square Garden on 23 January 1984 – **1,474 days**

8. Nuno Espírito Santo's run as Tottenham manager after replacing José Mourinho in 2021 – **125 days**

10. The 2022 Conservative leadership contest, which she won to become PM in the first place – **84 days**

Shorter than Liz Truss's reign as PM

1. David Blaine's 2003 'Above the Below' stunt, in which he was suspended over the River Thames in a Perspex box with no access to food – **44 days**

4. William Henry Harrison's time in office as the ninth president of the United States – **31 days**

5. The Anglo-Zanzibar War of 1896 – **38 minutes**

7. The construction of Mini Sky City, a fifty-seven-storey Chinese skyscraper that was completed in 2015 – **19 days**

9. Activist (and former *Have I Got News for You* panellist) Dan 'Swampy' Hooper's time spent in tunnels beneath the A30 in Devon, before being removed by police in 1996 – **7 days**

Spot the Fake Terrible Movie

2023 was a head-scratching year for film releases, with *Cocaine Bear* and *Winnie the Pooh: Blood and Honey* a) being greenlit, and b) receiving theatrical releases. Below are the titles and synopses of ten films, but only half of them are real. Can you work out which ones – against all odds – actually exist?

1. *The Gingerdead Man* – A witch bakes a serial killer's ashes into gingerbread spice mix, resulting in a sentient gingerbread man with a penchant for murder.
2. *Titanic II* – A replica of the *Titanic* sets sail to mark the one hundredth anniversary of the disaster, and suffers exactly the same fate as the original.
3. *Christ the Destroyer* – A freak astrological event causes Rio's famous *Christ the Redeemer* to come to life, wreaking havoc on anyone that crosses its path. Also, it can fly for some reason.
4. *Killer Sofa* – A disgraced rabbi and a voodoo sorceress come into possession of an evil reclining sofa, which goes on a bloody killing spree.
5. *Mr Hitler* – A school trip to Yellowstone National Park goes awry after students discover their new supply teacher is none other than Adolf Hitler.
6. *Mount Neverest* – A group of climbers fight for their lives after a zombie outbreak causes all of the dead bodies on Mount Everest to come back to life.

7. *The VelociPastor* – A Catholic priest is infected by an ancient Chinese artefact which causes him to turn into a dinosaur late at night.

8. *Frankenstein in Space* – The first manned mission to Mars hits an unexpected snag after a clerical mix-up sets Frankenstein's monster loose on a spaceship.

9. *Poltergay* – A house is haunted by five gay ghosts, owing to the basement being a former nightclub which burned down when a foam machine malfunctioned.

10. *Mega Shark vs Vest Beetle* – Humankind is powerless as two of nature's most deadly creatures go up against each other: a sixty-foot shark with human legs and arms, versus a regular-sized beetle that is wearing a vest.

Spot the Fake Terrible Movie – Answers

Real

1. *The Gingerdead Man* (2005)

2. *Titanic II* (2010)

4. *Killer Sofa* (2019)

7. *The VelociPastor* (2017)

9. *Poltergay* (2006)

Not real

3. *Christ the Destroyer*

5. *Mr Hitler*

6. *Mount Neverest*

8. *Frankenstein in Space*

10. *Mega Shark vs Vest Beetle*

With Russia's military supplies depleted by the ongoing war in Ukraine, the Kremlin deployed its new high-tech defence system to keep Putin safe from drone strikes:

2023 GENERAL KNOWLEDGE – ROUND 1

Cast your mind back, as these questions all relate to things that happened during the first few months of 2023.

1. Early in the year, the UK's most dim-witted inhabitants queued for hours to get their hands on an energy drink launched by YouTube 'celebs' KSI and Logan Paul, but what is it called?

    A. Grime
    B. Chime
    C. Prime
    D. Showtime

2. On 20 April one of Elon Musk's SpaceX Starships spectacularly exploded shortly after taking off from a launchpad in Texas. How was the explosion described by SpaceX's official Twitter account while debris was still raining from the sky?

    A. Unplanned rapid descent
    B. Premature uncoupling reaction
    C. Rapid unscheduled disassembly
    D. Sub-optimal flight-path deviation

3. In early February, tensions between the US and China increased significantly after what was spotted in the skies above Montana and South Carolina?

    A. Drone
    B. Satellite
    C. Missile
    D. Balloon

4. To celebrate International Women's Day 2023, Girlguiding advocates unveiled a statue depicting a female version of which historical figure?

    A. Winston Churchill
    B. Gandhi
    C. St George
    D. Jesus

5. One of 2023's bestselling video games – based on the Wizarding World of Harry Potter – made headlines for the entirely predictable culture war that followed its release on 7 February. What is it called?

    A. *Return to Hogwarts*
    B. *Hogwarts Legacy*
    C. *Quidditch Legends*
    D. *Voldemort's Revenge*

6. In an awkward moment at the 2023 Cheltenham Festival, which politician did Carol Vorderman run into after slating them on Twitter?

    A. Jeremy Corbyn

    B. Priti Patel

    C. Matt Hancock

    D. Nadhim Zahawi

7. In February an ad from Leicester-based insurance company DeadHappy was banned by the Advertising Standards Agency as it used the likeness of which British serial killer?

    A. Peter Sutcliffe

    B. Dennis Nilsen

    C. Fred West

    D. Harold Shipman

8. Actor-turned-vagina-candle-maker Gwyneth Paltrow became the subject of ridicule for an 11 March Instagram post promoting gloves that allegedly make it easier to do what?

    A. Brush your teeth

    B. Send text messages

    C. Masturbate

    D. Chop vegetables

9. Ahead of the League Cup Final on 26 February, Matt Hancock posted a video on TikTok of himself wearing a Newcastle United shirt. Why was this peculiar?

    A. Newcastle weren't playing in the final

    B. Matt Hancock supports Wigan Athletic

    C. He'd previously auctioned the shirt for charity

    D. Holes had been cut where his nipples were

10. On 10 March, why was minister for faux-outrage Lee Anderson ridiculed after tweeting 'Getting There. You won't see this in the MSM 👇👇'?

    A. He'd posted a broken link

    B. His tweet highlighted an MSM news article

    C. The article he linked to was from 2009

    D. He forgot to post a link altogether

2023 General Knowledge – Round 1 Answers

1. C – Shoppers fought over the viral energy drink Prime, with cases going for hundreds, sometimes thousands of pounds on eBay. It remains unclear what these people needed energy for though, as it doesn't appear there was much else going on in their lives.

2. C – SpaceX described the explosion as a 'rapid unscheduled disassembly', much in the same way that the Hindenburg experienced a rapid unscheduled deflation.

3. D – A spy balloon (because nothing says stealth quite like a forty-foot bag of air moving at two miles an hour) was spotted floating over the US, before eventually being shot down over the Atlantic Ocean. China initially feigned ignorance over the balloon but were forced to admit it was theirs after satellite images revealed 'HAPPY BIRTHDAY MR JINPING' written on the side.

4. C – The statue – which is in St John's Wood – is called *Georgina and the Dragon*. It received a mixed reception within the Girlguiding community, as dragon-slaying badges were phased out in the early 1970s.

5. B – *Hogwarts Legacy* was released to generally favourable reviews but was boycotted by some due to J.K. Rowling's views on trans rights, meaning the cash she made from it would only fill fifty Olympic swimming pools instead of fifty-one.

6. C – Carol Vorderman ran into Matt Hancock at the Cheltenham Festival after criticising his *I'm a Celebrity* appearance on Twitter. Eyewitnesses say they couldn't make out much of the conversation, but Vorderman called him something beginning with C, followed by a vowel and two consonants.

7. D – The ad – featuring Harold Shipman – received 115 complaints and was pulled for causing 'unjustified distress', as it overstated the chances of getting a GP appointment in 2023.

8. B – New-age goofball Gwyneth Paltrow took to Instagram to promote gloves that allegedly make it easier to send text messages, possibly in a desperate attempt to get her friends and family to speak to her.

9. C – Matt Hancock was wearing a shirt that he'd signed and auctioned off in 2020 to fund hospital scrubs for nurses (because as Health Secretary there was apparently no other way to procure them). He later revealed that the person who'd bought it (for a reported £1,850) had gifted it back to him, presumably as soon as the magic mushrooms wore off.

10. B – Lee Anderson claimed 'you won't see this in the MSM' and posted a screenshot of an article from a little-known local newspaper ... *The Times*. Which would have been a hugely embarrassing faux pas for anyone with a shred of self-awareness.

THE NICOLA STURGEON FISHY SURNAMES ROUND

Nicola Sturgeon shocked the world (well, a handful of people in Scotland) by resigning as first minister on 15 February. Wrangling ten questions out of her achievements was a bit of stretch, so instead the answers to this round are all people who – like Sturgeon – have aquatic surnames. Can you work them out from the clues below?

1. British film director and screenwriter, and two-time Palme d'Or winner, for *The Wind That Shakes the Barley* and *I, Daniel Blake*. Other credits include *Cathy Come Home* and *Kes*.

2. Presenter and actor whose credits include *Citizen Khan*, *Ackley Bridge* and *Good Morning Britain*. Is also a regular *Have I Got News for You* host.

3. Age-defying superhero actor who played Phoebe Buffay's love interest in the later seasons of *Friends*.

4. Veteran comedian and writer. Won the tenth series of *Taskmaster* and also came out on top in the subsequent *Champion of Champions* episode. Former comedy partner of Stewart Lee.

5. Oscar-nominated actress whose credits include *Gone Girl*, *Pride & Prejudice* and *Die Another Day*.

6. Gaffe-prone MP who bumbled his way through several cabinet positions, including a particularly calamitous run as transport minister between 2016 and 2019.

7. Former footballer who won the League Cup with Leicester, the Scottish league title with Celtic, and also had spells at Wycombe Wanderers, Port Vale, Stoke City and Leeds United.

8. American abstract expressionist painter, known for works created by dripping paint onto canvas.

9. Former US boyband member, whose hits include 'Bye Bye Bye', 'Tearin' Up My Heart' and 'It's Gonna Be Me'.

10. British actress who starred opposite Mark Wahlberg and Sir Anthony Hopkins in *Transformers: The Last Knight*.

The Nicola Sturgeon Fishy Surnames Round – Answers

1. Ken Loach

2. Adil Ray

3. Paul Rudd

4. Richard Herring

5. Rosamund Pike

6. Chris Grayling

7. Steve Guppy

8. Jackson Pollock

9. Lance Bass

10. Laura Haddock

PRETENTIOUS RED-CARPET OUTFITS OF 2023

For celebrities, awards ceremonies are about one thing and one thing only: looking as stupid as humanly possible in pursuit of column inches. 2023 didn't disappoint. Can you remember who wore the following atrocities of their own accord?

1.

2.

3.

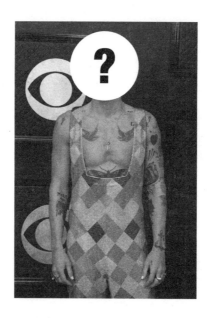

4.

5.

6.

Pretentious Red-Carpet Outfits of 2023 – Answers

1. Sam Smith (BRIT
Awards – 11 February)

2. Anya Taylor-Joy (BAFTA
Film Awards – 19 February)

3. Harry Styles
(Grammys – 5 February)

4. Shania Twain
(Grammys – 5 February)

5. Jared Leto
(Met Gala – 1 May)

6. Doja Cat (Paris Fashion
Week – 23 January)

THÉRÈSE COFFEY'S ROOT VEGETABLE WORDSEARCH

When the UK ran out of salad vegetables in February, world-renowned nutritionist and health expert Thérèse Coffey came to the rescue by suggesting that people eat turnips instead. Can you help Thérèse find all the ingredients for a slap-up meal?

1. Turnip
2. Radish
3. Rutabaga
4. Artichoke
5. Parsley
6. Carrot
7. Yam
8. Parsnip
9. Celeriac
10. Tragopogon

```
L E F R L S F S E W B T E I L R A D I S H I Y
D D N L W Y U C Q X Q J L I V C N S M S U T F
C N I L S C Q H G P A R S N I P E M F H J M Y
F V J O O B K K Y O Z R D Z B V Y Y O V I O M
P V M T N W G W G C R V U L R D T U R N I P H
T X A L D C R U U M Y Y R T V E U B Y Q I J T
P S Y F Z K A U I D U R I K A G O F Z J D I E
V M Z C Z E S S X A L N L M W B Q A J C N Y D
G L L H A D E K O H C I T R A Y A S D E D K J
N X F G Z C L U P C C M T F Y W G G G L H L X
Q N O G O P O G A R T F X H D Y M R A E Y A Z
E N A S E L T H E L W Y V E S O B R I R O P H
T O P A P Q U Q Y E L S R A P S M I F I A K K
N C A R R O T Y T I Z O W G B G M E G A O B D
V A B K N M H X X Z S N X T M Y M R R C O G E
U P J Q J G P Z X N M C M C B Y M L D M Y I Y
```

Thérèse Coffey's Root Vegetable Wordsearch – Solution

```
. . . . . . . . . . . R A D I S H . .
. . . . . . . . . . . . . . . . . .
. . . . . . . P A R S N I P . . . . .
. . . . . . . . R . . . . . . . . .
. . M . . . . . . . U . . . T U R N I P .
. . A . . . . . . . . T . . . . . . .
. . Y . . . . . . . . A . . . . . . .
. . . . . . . . . . B . . . C . . .
. . . . . E K O H C I T R A . A . . E . . .
. . . . . . . . . . . . . G . L . .
. N O G O P O G A R T . . . . . . A E . . .
. . . . . . . . . . . . . . . R . . .
. . . . . . Y E L S R A P . . . . I . . .
. C A R R O T . . . . . . . . . . A . .
. . . . . . . . . . . . . . . C . .
. . . . . . . . . . . . . . . . . .
```

Red wall support continued to crumble in 2023 after Rishi Sunak dropped his wallet during a visit to Hartlepool:

THE AI QUIZ ROUND

The biggest tech story of 2023 was unquestionably the rise of artificial intelligence, but while AI will almost definitely enslave the human race at some point in the future, can it write a decent quiz round? The answer is no, not really. The following round was produced by asking a chatbot to write multiple choice quiz questions based on politics, sport, history and geography. Good luck! You won't need it (at least, not for the first five questions . . .)

1. Which of the following people have never been British prime minister?

    A.   John Major

    B.   Ted Heath

    C.   Dale Winton

    D.   Theresa May

2. Muhammad Ali was a world champion in which sport?

    A.   Athletics

    B.   Cricket

    C.   Gymnastics

    D.   Boxing

3. Saddam Hussein served as president of which country between 1979 and 2003?

    A. Iraq

    B. Iran

    C. Iceland

    D. Jamaica

4. Which of the following rivers runs through London, England?

    A. Danube

    B. Thames

    C. Nile

    D. Yangtze

5. During the Apollo 11 spaceflight in 1969, who became the first man to set foot on the moon?

    A. Buzz Aldrin

    B. Michael Collins

    C. Neil Armstrong

    D. Ayrton Senna

By this point it was apparent that the questions were a bit on the easy side, so the prompt was adjusted with a request to make them more difficult. Apparently AI considers 'more difficult' to mean 'not out of place on a *Mastermind* specialist subject round'. Not sure we have to worry about a robot uprising just yet.

6. Which player scored two goals for Blackburn Rovers in the 1928 FA Cup Final?

    A. Jack Roscamp

    B. Herbert Jones

    C. Willie Rankin

    D. Austen Campbell

7. During the build-up to the Battle of Bosworth Field in 1485, Henry Tudor formed an alliance with which English knight shortly after heading east from Shrewsbury?

    A. Walter Herbert

    B. Bernard Stewart

    C. Gilbert Talbot

    D. John Howard

8. Which character injures their leg in Act V of William Shakespeare's *Othello*?

    A. Roderigo

    B. Brabantio

    C. Desdemona

    D. Cassio

9. Early in the sixteenth century, Portuguese settlers gained control of the Island of Mozambique after capturing which vital port city?

   A. Pemba
   B. Sofala
   C. Chimoio
   D. Maputo

10. Which of the following was named Best Documentary Feature at the thirty-first Academy Awards in 1959?

    A. *White Wilderness*
    B. *Antarctic Crossing*
    C. *The Hidden World*
    D. *Psychiatric Nursing*

THE AI QUIZ ROUND – ANSWERS

1. C – Dale Winton

2. D – Boxing

3. A – Iraq

4. B – Thames

5. C – Neil Armstrong

6. A – Jack Roscamp

7. C – Gilbert Talbot

8. D – Cassio

9. B – Sofala

10. A – *White Wilderness*

The World's Richest Idiot

Elon Musk spent 2023 doing his favourite things – working around the clock to get as much attention as humanly possible, and blowing things up (literally, in the case of his SpaceX rockets, and figuratively, in the case of Twitter). In July, *Forbes*'s Real Time Billionaires list placed his net worth at $237.7 billion, which is more than the GDP of some countries. Below are twenty nations, but are they worth more, or less, than Elon Musk?*

1. China
2. Greece
3. Hungary
4. South Korea
5. Croatia
6. Ukraine
7. Finland
8. Mexico
9. Switzerland
10. Iceland
11. San Marino
12. Paraguay
13. Vietnam
14. Egypt
15. Kenya
16. Belarus
17. Panama
18. Iraq
19. Portugal
20. United States

* According to PopulationU.com, as of July 2023

The World's Richest Idiot – Answers

Worth more than Elon Musk

1. China ($19.4 trillion)

2. Greece ($239.3 billion)

4. South Korea ($1.7 trillion)

7. Finland ($301.6 billion)

8. Mexico ($1.7 trillion)

9. Switzerland ($869.6 billion)

13. Vietnam ($449.1 billion)

14. Egypt ($387.1 billion)

18. Iraq ($267.9 billion)

19. Portugal ($267.7 billion)

20. United States ($26.8 trillion)

Worth less than Elon Musk

3. Hungary ($188.5 billion)

5. Croatia ($78.9 billion)

6. Ukraine ($148.7 billion)

10. Iceland ($28.6 billion)

11. San Marino ($1.8 billion)

12. Paraguay ($42.8 billion)

15. Kenya ($118.1 billion)

16. Belarus ($73.5 billion)

17. Panama ($77.2 billion)

True or False? – Round 1

The premise of this round is quite complicated, so pay attention. Below are twenty statements linked to 2023, but are they true or false?

1. For Valentine's Day 2023, Build-A-Bear Workshop launched a range of adult-only bears, complete with wine bottles, stilettos and sexy lingerie.
2. In May, a teacher in Kentucky, USA was suspended after allowing a student to dress up as a KKK grand wizard as part of a history project.
3. At a Q&A session ahead of the final season of *Succession*, producers revealed that Brian Cox had originally been their third choice for the role of Logan Roy, landing it only after Robert Redford and Michael Douglas had turned them down.
4. After being cleared of fault over a 2016 ski crash on 30 March, actress Gwyneth Paltrow was awarded just $1.
5. In a blog post on 6 April, street artist Banksy revealed that he had appeared on a UK game show under his real name but would never reveal which one or when it was.
6. In August, Edinburgh Zoo admitted that a koala bear escaped in 2015 and was on the loose for seven months before being captured on a farm sixteen miles away.
7. In January, an original Mr Blobby costume listed on eBay for £39 received a winning bid of £62,000 following a fierce bidding war.

8. In May, Plymouth City Council cut down a large number of trees to stop people having public sex in the area.

9. Blackpool council imposed a five-day ban on stag and hen dos in June following several cases of intoxicated donkey riding.

10. In April, police in Glasgow stopped a vehicle and discovered cocaine, heroin and a stowaway lamb sitting on the back seat.

11. In August, a branch of DFS in Wolverhampton issued a lifetime ban to a man who had been sleeping in the store every night for seven months.

12. In March, an Australian company announced that it had created a meatball made from the lab-grown flesh of a woolly mammoth.

13. The ISS had to receive advice from a plumber via video link in July after all four of the station's toilets stopped working.

14. Sotheby's withdrew an auction for a guitar that belonged to Jimi Hendrix in August after an inspection revealed a small bag of cocaine which had been sealed inside since 1970.

15. In May, the owner of an Australian bouncy castle firm was jailed for eleven years following a series of arson attacks on rivals.

16. In April, a Spanish woman broke the world record for living alone in a cave after spending five hundred days seventy metres below the earth's surface.

17. The BBC received nine complaints about an episode of *Gardeners' World* in February because Monty Don had grown a beard over the winter.

18. Madame Tussauds caved to pressure in April and removed waxworks of Osama bin Laden and Myra Hindley.

19. In April, Secret Service agents apprehended a toddler who had crawled through the security fence that surrounds the White House.

20. During a rerun of *The Crystal Maze* on Challenge TV in August, eagle-eyed viewers spotted that a contestant had cheated by storing homemade gold tickets inside his jumpsuit in order to win the grand prize.

True or False? – Round 1 Answers

True

1. For Valentine's Day 2023, Build-A-Bear Workshop launched a range of adult-only bears, complete with wine bottles, stilettos and sexy lingerie.

2. In May, a teacher in Kentucky, USA was suspended after allowing a student to dress up as a KKK grand wizard as part of a history project.

4. After being cleared of fault over a 2016 ski crash on 30 March, actress Gwyneth Paltrow was awarded just $1.

7. In January, an original Mr Blobby costume listed on eBay for £39 received a winning bid of £62,000 following a fierce bidding war.

8. In May, Plymouth City Council cut down a large number of trees to stop people having public sex in the area.

10. In April, police in Glasgow stopped a vehicle and discovered cocaine, heroin, and a stowaway lamb sitting on the back seat.

12. In March, an Australian company announced that it had created a meatball made from the lab-grown flesh of a woolly mammoth.

15. In May, the owner of an Australian bouncy castle firm was jailed for eleven years following a series of arson attacks on rivals.

16. In April, a Spanish woman broke the world record for living alone in a cave after spending five hundred days seventy metres below the earth's surface.

19. In April, Secret Service agents apprehended a toddler who had crawled through the security fence that surrounds the White House.

False

3. Robert Redford and Michael Douglas didn't turn down the role of Logan Roy.

5. Banksy didn't claim to have appeared on a British game show.

6. A koala bear didn't escape from Edinburgh Zoo in 2015.

9. Blackpool council didn't impose a five-day ban on stag and hen dos due to intoxicated donkey riding.

11. DFS didn't issue a lifetime ban to a man who'd been sleeping rough in their stores.

13. The ISS didn't have to receive advice from a plumber via video link in order to fix the station's toilets.

14 No bags of cocaine were discovered inside any of Jimi Hendrix's guitars.

17. The BBC didn't receive any complaints over Monty Don growing a beard. He remained as clean-shaven as ever.

18. Madame Tussauds didn't remove waxworks of Osama bin Laden and Myra Hindley, because they didn't exist in the first place.

20. *Crystal Maze* viewers didn't spot a cheating contestant on a rerun of an old episode.

Football Club Top Scorers

He might have played for one of the worst ever Premier League teams not to be relegated,* but he's got a round in a quiz book, so who's laughing now? Harry Kane became Tottenham Hotspur's all-time top scorer on 5 February after scoring his 267th goal for the club (which at the time worked out to around 268 goals per major trophy). He then also became England's top scorer on 24 March (again, no trophies). Can you work out the top scorers for each of the below clubs from their goal tallies and dates in which they were scored?

1. Barcelona – 672 goals, 2004–2021

2. Manchester United – 253 goals, 2004–2017

3. Arsenal – 228 goals, 1999–2007, 2012

4. Real Madrid – 450 goals, 2009–2018

5. Benfica – 473 goals, 1961–1975

6. Bayern Munich – 563 goals, 1964–1979

7. Rangers – 355 goals, 1983–1998

8. Chelsea – 211 goals, 2001–2014

9. Manchester City – 260 goals, 2011–2021

10. Santos – 643 goals, 1956–1974

* He moved to Bayern Munich in August, made his debut in the German Supercup and his new side were hammered 3–0 by RB Leipzig, so the wait for a trophy goes on . . .

Football Club Top Scorers – Answers

1. Lionel Messi

2. Wayne Rooney

3. Thierry Henry

4. Cristiano Ronaldo

5. Eusébio

6. Gerd Müller

7. Ally McCoist

8. Frank Lampard

9. Sergio Agüero

10. Pelé

MISSING WORDS – ROUND 1

All the fun of the *Have I Got News for You* missing words round but without the fear of Ian Hislop pressing you on shady business dealings from 2008. Can you complete the following headlines from the options below?

1. Spanish transport secretary resigns after new trains
    _____

    Guardian – 21 February

    A. Roll over in high winds
    B. Too big for tunnels
    C. Delivered to Venezuela
    D. Too long for platforms

2. Woman 'barred' from Lidl after buying _____ 'for business reasons'
    Daily Star – 22 February

    A. 15 machetes
    B. 250 energy drinks
    C. 40 leather whips
    D. 100 cucumbers

3. Mexican   president   claims   he   has   proof   of
   _____

   Telegraph – 26 February

      A.   Mythical woodland elf
      B.   Ancient aliens
      C.   Covid lab leak
      D.   JFK murder plot

4. Villagers set up electric fence after 'terrifying' _____
   causes thousands of pounds of damage
   Independent – 1 March

      A.   Sheep
      B.   Badger
      C.   Fox
      D.   Otter

5. Future of Britain's wonkiest _____ slides
   into uncertainty
   The Times – 9 March

      A.   Block of flats
      B.   Football pitch
      C.   Pub
      D.   Railway line

6. A 90-year-old _____ named Mr Pickles is a new dad of three
    New York Times – 22 March

    A. Tortoise
    B. Elephant
    C. Shark
    D. Tory peer

7. Italian soccer club hands lifetime ban to fan who wore _____ shirt to match
    Times of Israel – 22 March

    A. Homophobic
    B. Hitler
    C. X-rated
    D. Lewis Capaldi

8. Fan _____ in aisle near Hillary and Chelsea Clinton at Broadway show
    PageSix.com – 20 March

    A. Collapses
    B. Urinates
    C. Poops
    D. Strips nude

58

9. Russia beats Tom Cruise in race for first movie

Politico – 8 March

    A. With a continuous one-hour action sequence

    B. Filmed entirely underwater

    C. Shot in space

    D. Officially approved by the Church of Scientology

10. Jordan Peterson rails against 'tyranny' of

Independent – 25 February

    A. Four-slice toasters

    B. Antidepressants

    C. Paper towel dispenser

    D. Ribbed condoms

Missing Words – Round 1 Answers

1. B – Spanish transport secretary resigns after new trains **too big for tunnels**. On 20 February, Spain's secretary of state for transport, Isabel Pardo de Vera, resigned after it emerged that dozens of new trains were too wide to fit through some tunnels, although with a bit of perseverance and by slathering the carriages with olive oil they could just about get through.

2. D – Woman 'barred' from Lidl after trying to buy 100 **cucumbers** 'for business reasons'. During the great vegetable shortage of 2023, a forty-nine-year-old woman from Merseyside attempted to buy one hundred cucumbers, citing 'business reasons', and was promptly barred. To be fair though, if you've got one hundred cucumbers in your trolley then 'personal reasons' sounds even worse.

3. A – Mexican president claims he has proof of **mythical woodland elf**. President Andrés Manuel López Obrador tweeted a photo of what he claimed to be an ancient Mayan spirit, which – like all famous photos of the paranormal – was dimly lit, out of focus, and in truth looked like a raccoon with its head trapped in a carrier bag.

4. D – Villagers set up electric fence after 'terrifying' **otter** causes thousands of pounds of damage. Residents in the village of Martock in Somerset say they've lost fish worth thousands of pounds to the furry intruder. Environmentalists

say it might be linked to climate change, as it's unquestionably a little otter.

5. C – Future of Britain's wonkiest **pub** slides into uncertainty. The Crooked House – a pub described as Britain's wonkiest – was put up for sale in March. Due to mining work in the nineteenth century, the building was uneven throughout, meaning it was impossible to know whether you're pissed or not. (Britain's wankiest pub on the other hand is the Smashed Avocado in Islington.) The Crooked House would make headlines again later in the year when it burned down and was promptly demolished shortly after being sold to new owners.

6. A – A 90-year-old **tortoise** named Mr Pickles is a new dad of three. The tortoise – a resident of Houston Zoo, Texas – became the proud father of three hatchlings despite being born all the way back in 1943. His partner was just fifty-three years old at the time, making Mr Pickles the reptilian equivalent of Leonardo DiCaprio.

7. B – Italian soccer club hands lifetime ban to fan who wore **Hitler** shirt to match. The Lazio fan was punished for wearing a pro-Hitler shirt to a home game in March. Say what you will about fascists in Italian football, but at least they make the training run on time.

8. C – Fan **poops** in aisle near Hillary and Chelsea Clinton at Broadway show. A fellow audience member suffered an embarrassing moment at a performance of *Some Like it Hot* in March, with reports suggesting 'two turds' were discovered near the former first lady. It's a good job Bill wasn't with her, as he might have mistaken them for cigars.

9. C – Russia beats Tom Cruise in race for first movie **shot in space**. Russian film *The Challenge* was filmed aboard the International Space Station, something that Tom Cruise had previously expressed an interest in doing. Reviews of the film were lukewarm, mainly due to the lack of atmosphere.

10. C – Jordan Peterson rails against 'tyranny' of **paper towel dispenser**. Permanently outraged political commentator Jordan Peterson reacted furiously to a sign on a towel dispenser urging people to only use what they need, tweeting 'Up yours, woke moralists. Tyranny is always petty – and petty tyranny will not save the planet'. The towel dispenser has so far remained deafeningly silent on the matter. Typical woke coward.

ODD ONE OUT – ROUND 1

You know the drill: four things, but one doesn't belong. Half a point for the correct answer, and half for working out why. (Assuming you're playing for points with friends and family. If you're reading this alone while waiting to see the kids on Boxing Day, you can just skip straight to the answers if you want. Nobody will know, or care.)

1.

A: John Lydon

B: Cliff Richard

C: Celine Dion

D: Jedward

2.

A: Lenny Henry

B: Gavin Williamson

C: Stanley Johnson

D: David Attenborough

Odd One Out – Round 1 Answers

1. A – John Lydon is the odd one out. The others have all represented their countries at Eurovision (Cliff Richard – 1968 and 1973, Celine Dion – 1988, Jedward – 2011 and 2012) whereas Lydon – along with his band Public Image Ltd – failed in his attempt to represent Ireland at the 2023 contest, losing out to Wild Youth in a public vote on 4 February. Punk might not be dead, but Lydon's hopes of receiving nul points from a Moldovan weatherman certainly are.

2. C – It's Stanley Johnson who doesn't belong here, as Lenny Henry, Gavin Williamson and David Attenborough all have knighthoods. Johnson senior was controversially and (unsuccessfully) nominated by his son early in 2023, however, presumably for keeping the British aviation industry afloat during the pandemic.

Joe Biden gave a rousing speech during a summit with Japan and South Korea, which would have been even better if he'd been facing the lectern:

SPEED ROUND 1

Speed is the name of the game in this round (think Suella Braverman driving through a built-up residential area). You're against the clock so get out that timer. Each question has two possible answers, so if you're really competitive/a bit dim you could probably blag your way through. For incorrect answers add five seconds to your time. If you complete in less than ninety seconds you're a champion; ninety seconds to two and a half minutes makes you a thoroughbred; two and a half minutes to four minutes makes you a three-legged donkey; and any longer makes you a small pot of glue. Go!

1. Which Asian country hosted the 2023 G7 summit?

    Japan / Thailand

2. In June, the Green Party's sole MP announced that she would step down at the next general election. What is her name?

    Catherine Lamberton / Caroline Lucas

3. Elon Musk stepped down as the CEO of which social media company in June?

    Twitter / TikTok

4. Which member of the royal family is – as of 2023 – third in line to the throne?

Prince Edward / Princess Charlotte

5. Complete the 2023 film title: *Indiana Jones and the*

_____

Temple of Doom / Dial of Destiny

6. What type of vehicle was at the centre of the investigation into SNP funding at the start of the year?

Luxury yacht / Luxury motorhome

7. Rishi Sunak was fined by Lancashire Police on 21 January for committing which driving offence?

Speeding / Not wearing a seatbelt

8. In April, MP Andrew Bridgen was permanently expelled from the Conservative Party following comments comparing Covid vaccines to what?

Soviet Russia / The Holocaust

9. The final episode of *Succession* aired on 28 May. Which actor plays (or rather, played ...) the patriarch Logan Roy?

Brian Cox / Brian Blessed

10. In January Boris Johnson claimed that which world leader threatened him with a missile strike?

Vladimir Putin / Donald Trump

11. Which veteran British cyclist was forced to retire from the 2023 Tour de France after breaking his collarbone?

Chris Froome / Mark Cavendish

12. Recep Tayyip Erdoğan won the 2023 presidential election of which country?

Turkey / Bulgaria

13. Which British long-distance runner – who won two medals at the 2012 London Olympics – made their final marathon appearance in 2023?

Mo Farah / Paula Radcliffe

14. Which tennis player secured a record-breaking twenty-third grand slam in June after winning the French Open?

Rafael Nadal / Novak Djokovic

15. Jacinda Ardern resigned as prime minister of which country in January?

New Zealand / Australia

16. Which veteran Labour MP had the party whip removed in April for comments made about racism towards Jewish people in a letter to the *Observer*?

Diane Abbott / John McDonnell

17. Which animated US TV show celebrated its 750th episode on 21 May?

The Simpsons / *Family Guy*

18. In June which Australian singer scored her first top ten UK single since 2010 with 'Padam Padam'?

Natalie Imbruglia / Kylie Minogue

19. So-called 'influencer' Andrew Tate spent the first three months of 2023 behind bars in which European country?

Bulgaria / Romania

20. Which former boyband member broke the record for Scotland's biggest-selling stadium show in May after sixty-five thousand fans attended his concert at Murrayfield?

Harry Styles / Justin Timberlake

SPEED ROUND 1 – ANSWERS

1. Japan

2. Caroline Lucas

3. Twitter

4. Princess Charlotte

5. *Indiana Jones and the Dial of Destiny*

6. Luxury motorhome

7. Not wearing a seatbelt

8. The Holocaust

9. Brian Cox

10. Vladimir Putin

11. Mark Cavendish

12. Turkey

13. Mo Farah

14. Novak Djokovic

15. New Zealand

16. Diane Abbott

17. *The Simpsons*

18. Kylie Minogue

19. Romania

20. Harry Styles

YOU'LL NEVER SCORE NUL POINTS ALONE: EUROVISION COMES TO LIVERPOOL

In 2022 the UK achieved the unthinkable and actually received points at Eurovision, finishing second behind Ukraine, who – due to the ongoing Russian invasion – weren't able to host it (every cloud and all that). The UK could, however, and Liverpool became the first British city to host the competition since Birmingham in 1998 (and the BBC blew most of the next five years' entertainment budget on it). How much can you remember about the campest night of the year?

1.   First things first, who was the UK's entrant in 2023?

    A.   Mimi Webb

    B.   Mae Muller

    C.   Holly Humberstone

    D.   Shura

2. Although the contest was eventually awarded to Liverpool, which of the following British cities also made the final shortlist?

   A. Cardiff

   B. Glasgow

   C. Norwich

   D. Bristol

3. Which member of the royal family made a surprise appearance at the start of the show alongside last year's winners Kalush Orchestra?

   A. Queen Camilla

   B. Princess Beatrice

   C. Kate Middleton, Princess of Wales

   D. Prince Andrew

4. Graham Norton sacrificed the usual wit and sarcasm of his commentary to his cheerleading duties as host. Which other British TV personality took over in the commentary booth when he was on stage?

   A. Sue Perkins

   B. Nick Grimshaw

   C. Scott Mills

   D. Mel Giedroyc

5. Loreen became the first woman to win Eurovision twice, with power ballad 'Tattoo'. Which country did she represent?

    A. Sweden

    B. Finland

    C. Belgium

    D. Austria

6. Eurovision songs usually revolve around themes like love and heartbreak, but Austria's 2023 entry was solely dedicated to which nineteenth-century writer?

    A. Mark Twain

    B. Edgar Allan Poe

    C. Mary Shelley

    D. Oscar Wilde

7. Which British rock legend appeared during the show's interval, playing alongside Sam Ryder?

    A. Paul McCartney

    B. Roger Taylor

    C. Keith Richards

    D. Rob Halford

8. Each year, every competing country must nominate an official spokesperson who has to appear onscreen for all of thirty seconds and announce how their national jury voted. Who picked up the easiest pay cheque of their careers and revealed how the UK voted in 2023?

    A. Miranda Hart
    B. Rylan Clark
    C. Joe Lycett
    D. Catherine Tate

9. What did Croatian band Let 3 vow to do if they won?

    A. Perform the winner's reprise in the nude
    B. Buy a drink for everyone in the audience
    C. Destroy an effigy of Vladimir Putin with their guitars
    D. Send the trophy to President Zelenskyy

10. Although placing second on the night, Finland's entry – performed by rapper Käärijä – was the clear favourite inside the arena and was a viral hit across social media. Which traditional dance was the song named after?

    A. Viennese waltz
    B. Paso doble
    C. Foxtrot
    D. Cha-cha-cha

You'll Never Score Nul Points Alone: Eurovision Comes to Liverpool – Answers

1. B – Mae Muller represented the UK with 'I Wrote a Song' (which was actually created by a three-person writing team, but 'I Wrote a Song with Two Other People' isn't quite as catchy). After the dizzy heights of finishing second in 2022, normal service resumed as the UK finished second from last with just twenty-four points.

2. B – The other shortlisted host city was Glasgow, meaning thousands of Eurovision fans were deprived of experiencing the traditional Glaswegian greeting of a frenzied headbutt to the middle of the face.

3. C – The Princess of Wales played a brief piano solo during the start of the show, dressed in an elegant ballgown, and if that wasn't enough eye candy, the intro also included a cameo from Andrew Lloyd Webber.

4. D – Mel Giedroyc held the fort while Graham Norton had to appear onstage. Midway through the broadcast she appeared in the audience seductively churning butter, which Eurovision purists will know was a nod to a previous entrant, but to everyone else it just looked she was having a break-down. Nevertheless, it was still somehow one of the least camp moments of the broadcast.

5. A – Sweden's win was their seventh in the competition, pulling them level with Ireland, who last won the contest

in 1996 with Ted Crilly and Dougal McGuire's Europop anthem, 'My Lovely Horse'.

6. B – Austria's entry – by pop duo Teya & Salena – was an outwardly horny ode to Edgar Allan Poe, and (as is the case with most Eurovision songs) was far, far more horrifying than anything he ever put to paper.

7. B – For reasons that were never quite explained, Queen drummer Roger Taylor appeared with Sam Ryder while he reeled off one of his drab radio ballads, although to the untrained eye it looked like someone's grandad had got lost on the way to the toilets and ended up onstage.

8. D – Perhaps even more perplexing than Roger Taylor was Catherine Tate's selection as the UK's official spokesperson. Unlike most spokespeople on the night, she didn't reel off any of her catchphrases, although 'am I bovvered?' would have been quite appropriate for the majority of the UK when it comes to Eurovision.

9. A – Croatian band Let 3 (a group of middle-aged men who sang a satirical song taking aim at Vladimir Putin) vowed to perform the winner's reprise fully nude if they won. Fortunately for viewers, they placed thirteenth. The band has previously been fined for performing in the nude, despite their insistence that they weren't technically naked because they all had corks in their anuses (not a joke – this actually happened).

10. D – Finland's entry, performed by Käärijä, was called 'Cha Cha Cha'. The chorus was built around the lyrics 'Cha, cha, cha, cha, cha, cha, cha, ei', so fair play to him for remembering the words on the night.

ALL MIXED UP – ROUND 1

The following are all anagrams related to 2023. Can you unjumble them with help from the clues below?

1. ARSENAL NONFOOD (two words) – Veteran Formula 1 driver who secured a surprise podium in the opening race of the 2023 season at the Bahrain Grand Prix.

2. SERENELY UNOBSERVE (three words) – Religion-themed Channel 4 comedy that launched on 23 January, starring Simon Bird and Morgana Robinson.

3. TKO KIT (one word) – Social media app that was banned from government phones in March due to ongoing data concerns.

4. MANICAL (two words) – Italian football team that knocked Tottenham Hotspur out of the Champions League on 8 March.

5. ACCEDING NONI (three words) – Long-running reality TV show, won in 2023 by former gymnast Nile Wilson.

6. EFT PHRENSY (two words) – Veteran actor and broadcaster. Announced as host for the British version of *Jeopardy!*, which launched in late 2023.

7. FATSO SLEUTH (four words) – Video game adaptation that received rave reviews in early 2023, starring Pedro Pascal from *Game of Thrones* and Bella Ramsey from ... erm, *Game of Thrones*.

8. IRIS SUMO (one word) – Home state of Super Bowl LVII winners, the Kansas City Chiefs.

9. ANT COLDS (one word) – European country where BBC One's *The Traitors* is filmed.

10. MOHO MAINLANDS (two words) – Former *Big Brother* contestant who replaced Matt Lucas on *The Great British Bake Off* in 2023.

11. JAY TEES (one word) – British budget airline that announced the cancellation of one thousand seven hundred flights in July.

12. NEVILLE RD (one word) – *Lord of the Rings* location that was released as a colossal six-thousand-piece Lego set in March.

13. CARPOOL HEIST (two words) – Ancient Greek citadel which was forced to introduce crowd control policies in July due to a sharp increase in the number of tourists visiting the site.

14. AFRO LID (one word) – US state governed by 2024 presidential hopeful Ron DeSantis.

15. COLD WARTINESS (two words) – The UK's most-visited tourist attraction of 2022, as revealed in March.

16. LAMENTING WOK (two words) – Best Picture-nominated film at the 2023 Academy Awards, starring Frances McDormand, Ben Whishaw and Claire Foy.

17. MUCK SHEATH (two words) – Main (human) character of *Pokémon*. Was written out of the show in March after twenty-six years.

18. PIJIN XING (two words) – World leader with a striking resemblance to Winnie the Pooh. One of Vladimir Putin's only friends.

19. LEAKY BONFIRE (two words) – Veteran Scottish comedian who appeared in season fifteen of *Taskmaster* in 2023. Has also appeared on *Have I Got News for You* as both a panellist and host.

20. DECADE SPA (two words) – 2008 video game which received a next-gen remake in 2023. Takes place on the deserted spaceship USG *Ishimura* and involves shooting mutants until their legs fall off.

21. BANANA COPER (two words) – Spanish-French fashion designer who died in February at the age of eighty-eight.

22. NUT RELAXER (two words) – British rock frontman who headlined the Pyramid Stage at Glastonbury with his band in June.

23. STRINGY WOMB (two words) – League Two side that reached the quarter-finals of the FA Cup, eventually being knocked out by Brighton.

24. KAY WHEE (one word) – Marvel superhero played by Jeremy Renner, who was hospitalised in a snowplough accident on New Year's Day.

25. HURTLE (one word) – BBC crime drama that received the Netflix treatment in 2023. Stars Idris Elba in the lead role.

ALL MIXED UP – ROUND 1 ANSWERS

1. Fernando Alonso

2. *Everyone Else Burns*

3. TikTok

4. AC Milan

5. Dancing On Ice

6. Stephen Fry

7. *The Last of Us*

8. Missouri

9. Scotland

10. Alison Hammond

11. EasyJet

12. Rivendell

13. The Acropolis

14. Florida

15. Windsor Castle

16. *Women Talking*

17. Ash Ketchum

18. Xi Jinping

19. Frankie Boyle

20. *Dead Space*

21. Paco Rabanne

22. Alex Turner

23. Grimsby Town

24. Hawkeye

25. *Luther*

A military event in Woking came to an
abrupt halt after Michael Gove sneezed:

I Fought the Law, and the Law Mildly Inconvenienced Me

In April Donald Trump became the second US president to be arrested. (Many outlets reported that he was the first, but Ulysses S. Grant actually holds that distinction, having been nicked for speeding in a horse-drawn carriage way back in 1872.) Can you match the other famous faces below to the reason(s) for their arrest?

1. Winona Ryder

2. Justin Bieber

3. Hugh Grant

4. Matthew McConaughey

5. Martha Stewart

6. Bill Murray

7. Bruno Mars

8. Nicki Minaj

9. Anthony Worrall Thompson

10. Bill Gates

A. Possession of cocaine (2010)

B. Being high and naked while playing the bongos (1999)

C. Possession of a weapon with intent to use (2003)

D. Possession of marijuana (1970)

E. Shoplifting (2001)

F. Drink driving, resisting arrest, driving without a valid licence (2014)

G. Multiple driving offences (1975, 1977)

H. Insider trading (2003)

I. Lewd conduct in a public place (1995)

J. Shoplifting (2012)

I Fought the Law, and the Law Mildly Inconvenienced Me – Answers

1. E. Winona Ryder – Shoplifting (2001)

2. F. Justin Bieber – Drink driving, resisting arrest, driving without a valid licence (2014)

3. I. Hugh Grant – Lewd conduct in a public place (1995)

4. B. Matthew McConaughey – Being high and naked while playing the bongos (1999)

5. H. Martha Stewart – Insider trading (2003)

6. D. Bill Murray – Possession of marijuana (1970)

7. A. Bruno Mars – Possession of cocaine (2010)

8. C. Nicki Minaj – Possession of a weapon with intent to use (2003)

9. J. Anthony Worrall Thompson – Shoplifting (2012)

10. G. Bill Gates – Multiple driving offences (1975, 1977)

The Little Russian Tank that Could

Vladimir Putin was widely ridiculed in May after a single tank showed up to his hotly anticipated Victory Day Parade in Moscow. Can you help the awesome might of Russia's military find its way back to the Ukraine frontline by navigating the maze below?

THE LITTLE RUSSIAN TANK THAT COULD – SOLUTION

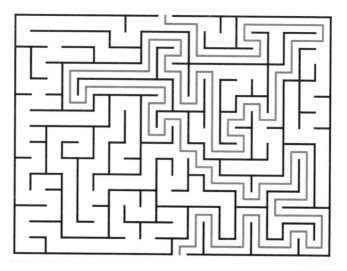

STRANGER THAN FICTION – ROUND 1

Below are ten sets of headlines. In each instance three are fake, but one is absolutely real and was published in 2023. Can you work out which ones are legit?

1. A. Researchers stumped by deep-sea octopus wearing a digital wristwatch

    B. Missing surfer alive and well after clinging to dolphin for nine hours

    C. Sea spiders can regrow lost anuses and sex organs – leaving scientists stunned

    D. Marine biologist's marriage saved by 'lucky' six-legged starfish

2. A. David Attenborough reunited with penguin that stole his wallet in 2006

    B. Cyclist 'lucky to be alive' after pigeon fractured his skull

    C. West Midlands Safari Park turns down £100k for its famous 'gay ostrich'

    D. Michael Bay denies killing a pigeon while shooting Netflix film in Italy

3. A. Amazon issues apology after dead cat posted through pensioner's letterbox

   B. Warning after Amazon customer sent dog food instead of iPhone

   C. Jeff Bezos personally delivers 100 millionth parcel to German grandfather

   D. Alexa records couple having sex, then plays it back during dinner party

4. A. Corgi-sized meteor as heavy as four baby elephants hits Texas – NASA

   B. Penis-shaped meteor leaves X-rated crater in Texas playing field

   C. Scientists disappointed as UFO revealed to be smudge on telescope lens

   D. NASA will pay you $100,000 to masturbate in space

5. A. Radio 2 DJ Sara Cox left red-faced after being caught short in a hot-air balloon

   B. Radio 1 DJ Greg James spends BRIT Awards trapped inside disabled toilet

   C. Radio 1 DJ Danny Howard saved by Ellie Goulding after choking on a Scotch egg

   D. Radio 2 DJ Scott Mills misses holiday after getting locked in car for five hours

6. A. Heinz giving new boat to man who survived at sea for twenty-four days on ketchup and spices

   B. Hellmann's issues apology following disastrous launch of mayonnaise-flavoured condoms

   C. Dolmio rewards man with jar-shaped head with lifetime supply of pasta sauce

   D. Heinz launches 'The Big One' – a single six-inch bean capable of feeding four people

7. A. National Park Service faces race against time as tourist gets head stuck in geyser

   B. Bear attacks fall by 60 per cent after Wyoming National Park bans obese tourists

   C. The real Yogi Bear? This nine-foot grizzly maimed a family and stole their picnic

   D. Pushing a 'slower friend' over and abandoning them isn't the best way to escape from a bear, National Park Service warns

8. A. Woman escapes from burning building by accident after chasing a boiled egg

   B. Boy Scout survives in wilderness for three days by eating his shoes

   C. US grandfather survives week in snowbank on croissants and biscotti

   D. Sole survivor of Himalayan plane crash signs lucrative plus-size modelling contract

9. A. Huge 160ft asteroid may smash into Earth on Valentine's Day 2046 ruining romantic plans

   B. Boffins say space may be smaller than previously thought following discovery of tennis ball on surface of moon

   C. Could hummingbirds hold the key to interstellar travel? Probably not, says one scientist

   D. Asteroid that wiped out the dinosaurs 'probably smelled strongly of egg'

10. A. Plane to Ibiza diverted after drunk passenger defecates in overhead luggage compartment

    B. Couple celebrating their honeymoon demand refund after all-inclusive package 'only includes crisps'

    C. Ryanair passenger questions value of in-flight scratch cards after paying £1 and winning 98p

    D. British holidaymaker reunited with dentures eleven years after vomiting them into a Benidorm bin

Stranger than Fiction – Round 1 Answers

1. C – Sea spiders can regrow lost anuses and sex organs – leaving scientists stunned (Sky News – 24 January). Now all that Covid stuff is (supposedly) out of the way, scientists can get back to the research that really matters, and in this case they made a huge breakthrough on the genitalia of sea spiders. What they haven't addressed however is how one 'loses' an anus, as historically, injuries to that area simply lead to a slightly bigger anus.

2. D – Michael Bay denies killing a pigeon while shooting Netflix film in Italy (*Rolling Stone* – 12 January). Legendary action director Michael Bay angrily hit back at reports that he'd shot a pigeon while filming a film called *6 Underground* for Netflix. In true Michael Bay fashion, the pigeon reportedly flipped sixteen times and exploded in slow motion.

3. B – Warning after Amazon customer sent dog food instead of iPhone (BBC News – 17 January). A sixty-nine-year-old man from Salisbury was shocked to discover the phone he'd ordered from the online retail giant was actually a packet of dog food, although probably not as surprised as the dog crunching its way through an iPhone 14.

4. A – Corgi-sized meteor as heavy as four baby elephants hits Texas – NASA (*Jerusalem Post* – 21 February). NASA unveiled their successor to imperial and metric measurements when a meteor 'the size of a Pembroke Welsh corgi and weighing around the total weight of four baby elephants'

crashed down in Texas in early February. Responders were able to reach the crash site in the time it takes to watch four episodes of *On the Buses*, and quickly cordoned off the resulting crater, which was the size of ninety tambourines.

5. D – Radio 2 DJ Scott Mills misses holiday after getting locked in car for five hours (*Independent* – 28 February). The veteran BBC DJ missed his flight to Amsterdam after the battery in his electric car died. Passers-by defended not breaking him out as the window was open and he had a bowl of water.

6. A – Heinz giving new boat to man who survived at sea for twenty-four days on ketchup and spices (Fox 13 – 28 February). After a sailor spent over three weeks adrift in the Caribbean Sea – surviving on nothing but tomato sauce and seasonings – ketchup giant Heinz tracked him down and offered to give him a new boat. Lee Anderson was quick to comment on the matter, as in his day people could survive twice as long at sea just by licking stamps.

7. D – Pushing a 'slower friend' over and abandoning them isn't the best way to escape from a bear, National Park Service warns (Insider – 2 March). This is objectively true, as in fact pushing your *fastest* friends into the bear's path gives you the best chance of survival, as the slow ones will be eaten regardless, although if you really want to get the job done you can also tie their shoelaces together.

8. C – US grandfather survives week in snowbank on croissants and biscotti (BBC News – 10 March). After getting caught up in snowstorms in northern California, eighty-one-year-old Jerry Jouret became trapped in his car and spent six days eating nothing but croissants and biscotti. He was

eventually hoisted out by a helicopter, which seems excessive, but by that point he probably weighed about forty stone.

9. A – Huge 160ft asteroid may smash into Earth on Valentine's Day 2046 ruining romantic plans (*Mirror* – 8 March). NASA said they were keeping an eye on an enormous asteroid that could potentially ruin your Valentine's Day, or if you're a bloke, get you off the hook by wiping out the planet before your wife realises your forgot to buy a card.

10. D – British holidaymaker reunited with dentures eleven years after vomiting them into a Benidorm bin (Sky News – 10 February). Spanish authorities returned the dentures to a sixty-three-year-old man from Greater Manchester after identifying him via a DNA database more than a decade after he spewed them into a bin during a drunken night out. The vomited gnashers are now on display at Ridge Hill Lane Working Men's Club in Stalybridge, in case anyone was looking for something to do with the kids at the weekend.

GOLDEN OLDIES

Old people had a decent showing in 2023. Judd Hirsch became the second-oldest actor to be nominated for an Oscar, Fernando Alonso enjoyed a Formula 1 comeback in his forties, and Joe Biden continued to bumble his way through world politics at the age of eighty. Therefore, the following questions are all about people who excelled in their advancing years. Can you guess who they are from just their achievements and initials?

1. TS – Oldest person to score a goal in the Premier League, netting for West Ham at the age of forty in a 2–1 defeat to Portsmouth in 2006.

2. JT – Oldest woman to win an acting Oscar – aged eighty – for 1989's *Driving Miss Daisy*.

3. BB – First woman to serve as Speaker of the House of Commons, elected at the age of sixty-two.

4. JC – Ultra-successful American TV chef and author whose first cookbook wasn't published until 1961, when she was forty-nine.

5. VW – Despite being one of the biggest names in fashion, she didn't enter the industry until 1987, when she was thirty-eight years old.

6. HM – British novelist who won the first of her two Booker Prizes at the age of fifty-seven for 2009's *Wolf Hall*.

7. SLJ – Nowadays one of Hollywood's most famous names, he didn't land his first major role until he was forty-three years old, in Spike Lee's 1991 romantic drama *Jungle Fever*.

8. TM – Oldest person to reach number one in the UK Singles Chart – at the age of ninety-nine – with a cover of 'You'll Never Walk Alone', released at the height of the Covid pandemic in 2020.

9. BW – Legendary television actress, who didn't receive her big break until she joined the cast of *The Mary Tyler Moore Show* in 1973 at the age of fifty-one.

10. TM – Author who in 1993 became the first African American woman to win the Nobel Prize for Literature, at the age of sixty-two.

Golden Oldies – Answers

1. Teddy Sheringham

2. Jessica Tandy

3. Betty Boothroyd

4. Julia Child

5. Vera Wang

6. Hilary Mantel

7. Samuel L. Jackson

8. Tom Moore

9. Betty White

10. Toni Morrison

General Knowledge – Round 2

Vladimir Putin allegedly takes part in a general knowledge quiz every morning – that is, to find out how many of his were blown up the previous day. Thankfully, these ten questions are much less macabre.

1. In late March, campaign group Led by Donkeys attempted to stitch up Matt Hancock, Kwasi Kwarteng, Gavin Williamson and Graham Brady by posing as a fake Korean firm and asking about advisory roles and access to other politicians. Which of the four MPs didn't take the bait and ended the call early?

   A. Matt Hancock
   B. Kwasi Kwarteng
   C. Gavin Williamson
   D. Graham Brady

2. On 5 April the Home Office deleted a tweet which described what as 'one of the greatest injustices in modern Britain'?

   A. The RNLI
   B. Human rights lawyers
   C. Exotic reptile smugglers
   D. Suella Braverman

3. During Prime Minister's Questions on 29 March, Dominic Raab paid tribute to a 'Paul Grayson'. Who was he referring to?

    A. Paul Simon

    B. Bono

    C. Paul O'Grady

    D. Paul Scholes

4. On 4 April environment minister Thérèse Coffey announced a near-total ban on what?

    A. Microbeads

    B. Wet wipes

    C. Rat poison

    D. Artificial lawns

5. At the launch of their new production company in March, Ben Affleck and Matt Damon revealed that they used to share what?

    A. Girlfriends

    B. Toothbrushes

    C. Baths

    D. A bank account

6. Who replaced Nicola Sturgeon as Scottish first minister on 29 March?

    A. Kate Forbes

    B. Humza Yousaf

    C. Ash Regan

    D. A potato

7. Why were organisers of the Razzies – a parody of the Oscars which honours the year's worst performances – forced to apologise after nominating actress Ryan Kiera Armstrong for her role in the film *Firestarter*?

    A. She wasn't in the film

    B. They nominated her in the male actor category by accident

    C. She had specifically asked to be omitted

    D. She was only twelve years old

8. In January the Japanese government announced plans to release millions of tonnes of what into the ocean?

    A. Radioactive water

    B. Genetically modified fish

    C. Plastic-eating plankton

    D. Raw sewage

9. In March it was revealed that Keir Starmer hoped to appoint which controversial figure as his new chief of staff?

   A. Simon Case
   B. Nick Timothy
   C. Dominic Cummings
   D. Sue Gray

10. When Grant Shapps tweeted a picture of himself at Cornwall's new spaceport on 10 January, eagle-eyed sleuths discovered that someone had been airbrushed out. Who was it?

   A. Liz Truss
   B. Matt Hancock
   C. Boris Johnson
   D. Nadine Dorries

General Knowledge – Round 2 Answers

1. C – Despite often being the bluntest knife in the drawer, Gavin Williamson was the only one of the four who smelled a rat with the non-existent company's offer. 1922 Committee chairman Sir Graham Brady suggested a daily rate of six thousand pounds, which is quite ambitious for someone whose only purpose is to open an envelope once every six months.

2. D – The unfortunately worded tweet read 'It's time to put an end to one of the greatest injustices in modern Britain. The Home Secretary, @SuellaBraverman' and was swiftly deleted, but like every other embarrassing thing on the internet, it was screenshotted and reposted so many times that it would have been seen by fewer people if they'd just left it up.

3. C – Raab was talking about (or rather, attempting to talk about) TV presenter Paul O'Grady, who had died the previous day. Neither Rishi Sunak or Keir Starmer were present at the PMQs in question, which resulted in a showdown between Raab and Angela Rayner. Fischer vs Spassky eat your heart out.

4. B – Thérèse Coffey announced a ban on wet wipes (the third time the government had put forward such proposals since 2018). Upon hearing the news, Dominic Raab let out a sigh and began clearing his desk.

5. D – Affleck and Damon revealed that they shared a bank account when they were younger. Perhaps that's where Harry Redknapp and his dog got the idea.

6. B – After a leadership contest that made last year's Tory one seem like the most exciting thing that has ever happened, Humza Yousaf beat Kate Forbes with 52 per cent of the vote, which as anyone in the UK will tell you is the magic number for settling any important issue once-and-for-all.

7. D – The organisers of the Razzies apologised because Ryan Kiera Armstrong was only twelve years old. Drew Barrymore – a former child actor who had played the same role in the 1980s – slammed the nomination and it was promptly withdrawn, with an apology which itself was worthy of a worst acting trophy.

8. A – The plan to release millions of tonnes of radioactive water from the Fukushima nuclear plant was announced by Japanese scientists, who have presumably never seen a Godzilla film.

9. D – Sue Gray resigned from the civil service in March with an aim to become the Labour leader's new chief of staff. Rules dictate that senior civil servants must wait at least three months before accepting outside employment, which is lucky as that's how long it took her to fill out the application form.

10. C – Boris Johnson had been edited out of the photo. The *Guardian* said the former PM had been replaced with 'a gaping hole', which some would argue is a like-for-like swap.

At the Scottish Labour conference in Edinburgh, Keir Starmer proudly announced how many policies he'd come up with since becoming leader:

NAME THAT CHANCELLOR

In the thirty years since May 1993 the UK has had ten chancellors of the exchequer, although incredibly, half of those have been in office since 2019. Going backwards in chronological order, can you work out the most recent chancellors from the clues below?

1. *(October 2022–present)* A ministerial journeyman whose surname is often mispronounced during live television broadcasts, sometimes accidentally.

2. *(September 2022–October 2022)* Appointed by Liz Truss and immediately crashed the economy with a disastrous 'mini budget'. The alleged intellectual heavyweight was sacked at 36,000ft while flying home from the US.

3. *(July 2022–September 2022)* Appointed by Boris Johnson, only to withdraw his support for the PM forty-eight hours later. His tax affairs while he was chancellor would come under heavy scrutiny in early 2023.

4. *(February 2020–July 2022)* Mega-wealthy chancellor who balanced his time between angling for the top job, posing for awkward photographs and convincing people that it was safe to go out for lunch in a pandemic.

5. *(July 2019–February 2020)* Billiard ball-headed former banker who has bounced around several ministerial jobs without ever really making much of an impact. Teamed up with his successor in 2022 to spark the sequence of events that led to Boris Johnson's resignation.

6. *(July 2016–July 2019)* Long-serving Conservative MP (and, by modern standards, a long-serving chancellor) who sat out his last few months as an independent after voting against Boris Johnson's government. Shares a surname with a pint-sized motoring journalist.

7. *(May 2010–July 2016)* Man of a thousand jobs (and barely qualified for any). Formerly editor of the *Evening Standard*, and now – incredibly – chair of the British Museum.

8. *(June 2007–May 2010)* Labour chancellor who assumed the role when his predecessor became PM. For fans of pretentious British titles that mean absolutely nothing, he is also referred to – by himself at least – as the Baron of Roulanish.

9. *(May 1997–June 2007)* Longest-serving post-war chancellor (by quite a margin) and ray of sunshine who was rewarded with a brief stint as PM. Nowadays mainly pops up on Sunday morning TV to slag off Brexit.

10. *(May 1993–May 1997)* Former Father of the House and smoking enthusiast who tried – and failed – to become leader of the Conservative Party on three separate occasions. Fiercely pro-European throughout his career, and was the only Conservative MP to vote against triggering Article 50 in 2017.

NAME THAT CHANCELLOR – ANSWERS

1. Jeremy Hunt

2. Kwasi Kwarteng

3. Nadhim Zahawi

4. Rishi Sunak

5. Sajid Javid

6. Philip Hammond

7. George Osborne

8. Alistair Darling

9. Gordon Brown

10. Kenneth Clarke

TRUE OR FALSE? – ROUND 2

Twenty more outlandish statements about 2023, but are they true or false?

1. In March, former Brazilian president Jair Bolsonaro travelled from Orlando to Brasília on a Harry Potter-themed plane.
2. Archbishop of Canterbury Justin Welby received three points on his driving licence in May after being caught speeding in a Volkswagen Golf.
3. During a world record attempt on 9 April, the construction of a sixty-foot-tall Easter egg was halted after a Belgian chocolatier fell into it.
4. In April, a pair of leather shorts belonging to Freddie Mercury sold at auction for £18,000.
5. In August, Keele University raised £600 for charity after auctioning off a urinal used by David Beckham.
6. A disagreement between political and religious authorities in March resulted in Lebanon being in two different time zones at the same time.
7. In May, researchers announced that the weight of New York's skyscrapers is causing Manhattan to slowly sink into the sea.
8. In June, Kiss bass player Gene Simmons attended PMQs as a guest of DUP MP Ian Paisley.

9. A garden centre in Morecambe was forced to close for two weeks in January after two of their workers who had played Santa Claus over the festive season tested positive for Legionnaires' disease.

10. In March, wildlife experts claimed that British eels were aiding Putin's war in Ukraine as Russian conservation projects were selling them on to China as food.

11. In April, police in Milan unveiled a Lamborghini patrol car and immediately wrote it off while demonstrating its features to members of the press.

12. In March, researchers announced that a piece of tartan discovered in a bog in the 1980s was in fact the oldest-known piece of tartan in the world, dating back to the sixteenth century.

13. Japanese authorities were forced to crack down on so-called 'sushi terrorism' in 2023, including the arrest of two men in April who were caught dipping their own chopsticks into a communal bowl of pickled ginger.

14. In July, complications from a faecal matter transplant caused Kerry Katona to grow a fingernail on her elbow.

15. A Toyota Corolla that had previously been owned by Keith Chegwin failed to sell at an auction in August, despite only having a reserve of £250.

16. In September, Tesco quietly changed the name of their Granny Smith apples to green delights, claiming that the previous name was 'ageist'.

17. A new-build housing estate in Truro was forced to replace four hundred windows after local residents complained that they were shaped like penises.

18. In June, a seventy-six-year-old Ecuadorian woman woke up during her own funeral and began banging on the inside of the coffin.

19. Toronto's 2023 mayoral election boasted a field of 102 candidates, one of which was a dog.

20. At the 2023 European Athletics Team Championships, a Belgian shot-putter stepped in for an injured teammate and took part in the 100-metre hurdles, finishing nineteen seconds behind the rest of the field.

TRUE OR FALSE? – ROUND 2 ANSWERS

True

1. In March, former Brazilian president Jair Bolsonaro travelled from Orlando to Brasília on a Harry Potter-themed plane.

2. Archbishop of Canterbury Justin Welby received three points on his driving licence in May after being caught speeding in a Volkswagen Golf.

4. In April, a pair of leather shorts belonging to Freddie Mercury sold at auction for £18,000.

6. A disagreement between political and religious authorities in March resulted in Lebanon being in two different time zones at the same time.

7. In May, researchers announced that the weight of New York's skyscrapers is causing Manhattan to slowly sink into the sea.

8. In June, Kiss bass player Gene Simmons attended PMQs as a guest of DUP MP Ian Paisley.

10. In March, wildlife experts claimed that British eels were aiding Putin's war in Ukraine as Russian conservation projects were selling them on to China as food.

12. In March, researchers announced that a piece of tartan discovered in a bog in the 1980s was in fact the oldest-known

piece of tartan in the world, dating back to the sixteenth century.

13. Japanese authorities were forced to crack down on so-called 'sushi terrorism' in 2023, including the arrest of two men in April who were caught dipping their own chopsticks into a communal bowl of pickled ginger.

18. In June, a seventy-six-year-old Ecuadorian woman woke up during her own funeral and began banging on the inside of the coffin.

19. Toronto's 2023 mayoral election boasted a field of 102 candidates, one of which was a dog.

20. At the 2023 European Athletics Team Championships, a Belgian shot-putter stepped in for an injured teammate and took part in the 100m hurdles, finishing nineteen seconds behind the rest of the field.

False

3. A Belgian chocolatier didn't fall into a giant Easter egg.

5. Keele University didn't auction off a urinal used by David Beckham.

9. A Morecambe garden centre wasn't forced to close due to its Santa Claus actors contracting Legionnaires' disease.

11. Police in Milan didn't write off a Lamborghini patrol car moments after unveiling it.

14. Kerry Katona didn't grow a fingernail on her elbow as a result of a faecal matter transplant gone wrong.

15. A Toyota Corolla owned by Keith Chegwin never went to auction.

16. Tesco didn't change the name of their Granny Smith apples to green delights.

17. No housing estates in Truro were forced to replace windows due to complaints that they were shaped like penises.

BADLY CROPPED GUEST HOSTS

The following photos are all of people who have hosted *Have I Got News for You* in 2023, but quality control has dropped off a bit with regards to the cropping. Can you work out who they are from the following portions of their upper half?

1.

2.

1.

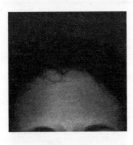

4.

5.

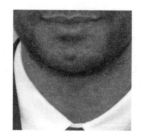

6.

BADLY CROPPED GUEST HOSTS – ANSWERS

1. Harry Hill

2. Naga Munchetty

3. Mel Giedroyc

4. Diane Morgan

5. Richard Ayoade

6. Charlie Brooker

Toy (Hi)Story

One of the most unexpected cultural showdowns of 2023 occurred in July when Greta Gerwig's *Barbie* and Christopher Nolan's *Oppenheimer* opened on the same day, both to critical acclaim. The following (completely fictional) scenarios involve a classic child's toy and a historical event. Can you name both? (And no half points, it's all or nothing.)

1. 1348. A robotic, owl-like creature dances (wobbles) onto a ship en route to Dorset and infects a sailor.

2. 1969. A man straps on a pair of very springy shoes, steps outside, and jumps twenty feet in the air.

3. Early sixteenth century. An Italian artist struggles to accurately illustrate his subject's enigmatic smile as he's limited to twisting two knobs that only produce vertical and horizontal lines.

4. 1966. A highly anticipated football match gets off to a slow start as all the players have the bottom third of a sphere attached to their feet.

5. 2008. A British racing driver defies the odds and wins his first world title in a yellow and red car which he powers with his legs.

6. 1989. A wall built with small plastic bricks is dismantled.

7. 1861. A Confederate soldier expresses concern about the stopping power of his pump-action water pistol.

8. 2500 BC. The building of a large shape is made easier by a man who can extend his arms to twice the length of his body.

9. 1953. A royal ceremony is interrupted by a small red guest who won't stop giggling.

10. 1974. An American politician resigns after being caught feeding balls to sub-Saharan semiaquatic mammals.

TOY (HI)STORY – ANSWERS

1. Furby and the Black Death

2. Moon boots and the moon landing

3. Etch-a-Sketch and the painting of the Mona Lisa

4. Subbuteo and the 1966 World Cup Final

5. Cozy Coupe and Lewis Hamilton's first world title win

6. Lego and the fall of the Berlin Wall

7. Super Soaker and the American Civil War

8. Stretch Armstrong and the building of the Great Pyramid

9. Tickle Me Elmo and the coronation of Queen Elizabeth II

10. Hungry Hungry Hippos and the resignation of Richard Nixon

Who Said It: Greta Thunberg or Optimus Prime?

One is a climate change activist, the other – rather conversely – transforms into a massive truck, but both have a penchant for dramatic speeches about saving the planet. Can you work out which of the following quotes are from Greta Thunberg and which are from Autobots leader Optimus Prime?

1. 'You are going to face justice, and may it be kinder to you than it was to us.'
2. 'Hope is telling the truth. Hope is taking action. And hope always comes from the people.'
3. 'We can't save the world by playing by the rules, because the rules have to be changed.'
4. 'Fate rarely calls upon us at a moment of our choosing.'
5. 'Entire ecosystems are collapsing. We are in the beginning of a mass extinction.'
6. 'At the heart of every legend there is truth; a few brave souls unite to save the world. We can be heroes in our own lives, every one of us, if we only have the courage to try.'
7. 'We will not understand it until it's too late. And yet we are the lucky ones.'
8. 'I fight for my own kind. My own planet!'
9. 'Either we choose to go on as a civilisation or we don't. That is as black or white as it gets.'
10. 'There's a thin line between being a hero and being a memory.'

Who Said It: Greta Thunberg or Optimus Prime? – Answers

1. Optimus Prime
   Transformers: Megatron's Master Plan (1985)

2. Greta Thunberg
   28 September 2021

3. Greta Thunberg
   24 November 2018

4. Optimus Prime
   Transformers: Revenge of the Fallen (2009)

5. Greta Thunberg
   23 September 2019

6. Optimus Prime
   Transformers: The Last Knight (2017)

7. Greta Thunberg
   23 April 2019

8. Optimus Prime
   Transformers: The Last Knight (2017)

9. Greta Thunberg
   25 January 2019

10. Optimus Prime
    Transformers: More Than Meets the Eye (1984)

I Fancy a Career Change . . .

Volodymyr Zelenskyy continued to dominate headlines in 2023 as he led Ukraine's defence against Russia's waning 'special military operation', but, as you probably know, prior to becoming a politician he was a successful comedian. From the following clues and initials, can you name these twenty famous people who – with varying levels of success – also decided to enter the world of politics?

1. Muscle-bound star of *The Terminator* and *Last Action Hero* who served as the thirty-eighth governor of California between 2003 and 2011. (AS)

2. Cricketer who took 362 Test wickets during a twenty-one-year career, before becoming president of Pakistan in 2018. (IK)

3. *Sex and the City* actress who (unsuccessfully) attempted to become governor of New York in 2018. (CN)

4. Multi-time boxing champion, and the first to win world titles in eight different weight divisions. Lost to Floyd Mayweather in 2015's so-called 'Fight of the Century', which was the highest-grossing pay-per-view in history, generating $410 million in revenue. In 2016 he was elected to the Philippines senate, and in 2022 placed third in the country's presidential election. (MP).

5. The only person to have served as both president of the Screen Actors Guild and president of the United States of America. (RR)

6. 1930s child actress who would go on to serve as the United States ambassador to both Czechoslovakia and Ghana, as well as chief of protocol under Gerald Ford. Shares a name with a non-alcoholic cocktail which is traditionally made with ginger ale and grenadine. (ST)

7. Found fame in a singing duo with his wife (a little-known artist known as Cher) in the 1960s and would later become a member of the House of Representatives from 1995 until his death in 1998. (SB)

8. British comedian with a pub-landlord gimmick who founded the Free United Kingdom Party (FUKP) and ran against Nigel Farage at the 2015 general election (neither were elected). (AM)

9. Former footballer who played for AC Milan, Chelsea and Manchester City, and went on to become the twenty-fifth president of Liberia in 2018. (GW)

10. English television personality who presented *That's Life!* between 1973 and 1994. Stood as an independent candidate at the 2010 general election, where she only secured 4 per cent of the vote. (ER)

11. Former reality TV host who served as US president between 2017 and 2021, and hopes to secure a second stint in 2024. (DT)

12. Notorious Welsh drug smuggler and author who contested four seats at the 1997 UK general election on the single issue of cannabis legalisation. (HM)

13. Four-time Olympic medallist who served as the Conservative MP for Falmouth and Camborne from 1992 to 1997. His association with the Olympics was revived in the following decade as he headed the 2012 London Olympic bid. (SC)

14. Another Olympic medallist, and former stepfather to Kim Kardashian. Underwent gender transition in 2015, and is often targeted by *South Park* due to her questionable driving record. (CJ)

15. Former war reporter and UNICEF ambassador who famously unseated Neil Hamilton at the 1997 general election, despite standing as an independent candidate. (MB)

16. Flamboyant WWF wrestler who had world title bouts with Hulk Hogan and Bob Backlund. Served as the thirty-eighth Governor of Minnesota between 1999 and 2003. (JV)

17. Veteran (ancient) US actor, who has appeared in dozens of films including *Dirty Harry*, *Where Eagles Dare* and *Million Dollar Baby*. Was elected as the mayor of Carmel-by-the-Sea, California in 1986, whereupon he made it legal to consume ice cream on city streets. He also famously empty-chaired Barack Obama at the 2012 Republican National Convention. (CE)

18. Former Fugees member who tried to run for president of Haiti in 2010, but was rejected due to having not lived in the country for five years prior to the election. (WJ)

19. Comedian and writer who enjoyed a successful stint on *Saturday Night Live* before going on to become United States senator for Minnesota from 2009 to 2018. (AF)

20. Extremely irritating US rapper who held rallies in 2020 ahead of a proposed presidential campaign. Has since announced that he'll be running in 2024 instead, despite controversial comments about slavery and Adolf Hitler, which resulted in him losing a hugely lucrative partnership with Adidas. (KW)

I Fancy a Career Change . . . Answers

1. Arnold Schwarzenegger

2. Imran Khan

3. Cynthia Nixon

4. Manny Pacquaio

5. Ronald Reagan

6. Shirley Temple

7. Sonny Bono

8. Al Murray

9. George Weah

10. Esther Rantzen

11. Donald Trump

12. Howard Marks

13. Sebastian Coe

14. Caitlyn Jenner

15. Martin Bell

16. Jesse Ventura

17. Clint Eastwood

18. Wyclef Jean

19. Al Franken

20. Kanye West

THE 2023 FILES

In March, tens of thousands of WhatsApp messages sent by Matt Hancock at the peak of the Covid pandemic were leaked to the *Daily Telegraph* and laid bare the government's complete and utter ineptitude in dealing with the crisis. Below are five (completely made up) text exchanges, but can you work out which 2023 news stories they're referencing?

1. (4 September)

> **Gillian**: Hi . . . so erm, I've just done an interview with ITV and . . . are you sitting down?

Rishi: Yes . . . on my arse, 'doing nothing' 😠

2. (23 August)

> **Vladimir**: Are you all set?

Yevgeny: There's a strange beeping noise . . . perhaps someone's alarm clock?

> **Vladimir**: I'm sure it's nothing – have a safe flight! ✈️

3. (20 August)

> **Jill**: I really think we need to visit. It's been almost a fortnight

Joe: screen too dark on cell phone. how I turn up brightness ? ?

> **Jill**: Perhaps we could fly out on Saturday? To show our support?

Joe: ,,,,Siri, how to turn up brightness,,,, screen too dark ? ?p

4. (18 June)

> **Stockton**: Hi yes, we've run into a spot of bother and require assistance

RAC Customer Support: Can I please take your location and we'll get a driver to you ASAP ☺

> **Stockton**: Wonderful. According to Google Maps we're about 370 miles off the coast of Newfoundla . . .

5. (1 February)

        Jeremy: Half a million people,
        what a turnout! Want me
        to join the picket line?

Mick: That'd be great, we're
protesting in Kensington

        Jeremy: Wonderful, I'll just hop
        on the train and ... oh ☹

THE 2023 FILES – ANSWERS

1. Education Secretary Gillian Keegan is recorded by ITV News complaining that nobody ever congratulates MPs for a job well done while others just sit around on their arses doing nothing.

2. Yevgeny Prigozhin's private jet falls out of the sky less than two months after the Wagner Group – on his orders – marched on Moscow.

3. Joe Biden finally decides to visit Hawaii two weeks after large parts of the US state were ravaged by wildfires.

4. The OceanGate *Titan*'s ill-fated journey to the wreck of the *Titanic*.

5. Britain hit by the biggest day of strikes in over a decade, with an estimated half a million workers taking part in a mass walkout.

Queen Camilla became the latest member of the royal family to be immortalised by Madame Tussauds:

CENSORED!

In February, Roald Dahl's books were 'updated' once again, in order to make them more palatable to modern audiences (honestly, if you can't laugh at a fat German child drowning in chocolate, what can you laugh at?). Below are ten famous lines from books, but they've been partially censored. Can you name the works that they appear in?

1. 'But soft! What light through ███████████? It is the East, and ████ is the sun.'

2. 'Very few ████████ can claim to have survived so long ████ as Mr. Patel, and none in the company of an ████ ████████.'

3. '█████ Ishmael.'

4. 'The answer to the ultimate question ████████ ████████ 42.'

5. 'And so we beat on, ████ against the ██████, borne back ceaselessly into the past.'

6. 'And may ███████████ in your favour.'

7. 'As ███████████████████████ from uneasy dreams he found himself transformed in his bed into an ████████████.'

8. 'The creatures outside looked from ███████, and from ████████, and from ████████ again; but already it was impossible to say which was which.'

9. 'Every Who down in ████████ liked ████████ a lot ... But the ██████, who lived just north of ███████, did NOT!'

10. 'It was the ████████, it was the ██████████, it was the ██████████, it was the ████████████, it was the ██████████, it was the ██████████████, it was the season of light, it was the ████████████, it was the ██████████, it was the ██████████.'

Censored! – Answers

1. 'But soft! What light through yonder window breaks? It is the East, and Juliet is the sun.'

   Romeo and Juliet, William Shakespeare

2. 'Very few castaways can claim to have survived so long at sea as Mr. Patel, and none in the company of an adult Bengal Tiger.'

   Life of Pi, Yann Martel

3. 'Call me Ishmael.'

   Moby-Dick, Herman Melville

4. 'The answer to the ultimate question of life, the universe and everything is 42.'

   The Hitchhiker's Guide to the Galaxy, Douglas Adams

5. 'And so we beat on, boats against the current, borne back ceaselessly into the past.'

   The Great Gatsby, F. Scott Fitzgerald

6. 'And may the odds be ever in your favour.'

   The Hunger Games, Suzanne Collins

7. 'As Gregor Samsa awoke one morning from uneasy dreams he found himself transformed in his bed into an enormous insect.'

The Metamorphosis, Franz Kafka

8. 'The creatures outside looked from pig to man, and from man to pig, and from pig to man again; but already it was impossible to say which was which.'

Animal Farm, George Orwell

9. 'Every Who down in Whoville liked Christmas a lot . . . But the Grinch, who lived just north of Whoville, did NOT!'

How the Grinch Stole Christmas!, Dr. Seuss

10. 'It was the best of times, it was the worst of times, it was the age of wisdom, it was the age of foolishness, it was the epoch of belief, it was the epoch of incredulity, it was the season of light, it was the season of darkness, it was the spring of hope, it was the winter of despair.'

A Tale of Two Cities, Charles Dickens

All Mixed Up – Round 2

More people or things that made headlines in 2023, but they've been mixed up. How many can you unscramble?

1. CAMEL TAIL (one word) Ageing US rockers who scored their first number-one album in the UK since 2008 with *72 Seasons* in April, and also headlined two separate nights at the 2023 Download Festival at Castle Donington.

2. COSTUMIER (two words) Action star who performs his own stunts. Appeared in 2023's *Mission: Impossible – Dead Reckoning Part One*.

3. ROTTEN TOKENS (three words) City in Staffordshire that is famous for its pottery. In June it was rocked by a magnitude three earthquake

4. FRAG KANGAROO WÖRD (four words) Norse mythology-based video game which received a record fifteen nominations at the 2023 British Academy Games Awards.

5. DERK FLAGELLAR (two words) German fashion designer. Died in 2019 but was honoured at the 2023 Met Gala by celebrities wearing extremely stupid outfits.

6. ACFERN (one word) Host nation for the 2023 Rugby World Cup.

7. ALLENTOWN FREQUENT THEORIST (six words) Winner of Best International Feature Film at the 2023 Academy Awards. Follows a young German soldier during the last days of the First World War, and is based on a 1929 novel of the same name.

8. GLIB THUD (two words) American beer brand which saw its stock price tumble by 20 per cent after partnering with transgender influencer Dylan Mulvaney in April.

9. ELWIN JOSH (two words) British department store that specialises in mawkish Christmas adverts. Came under fire in June for plans to build ten thousand rental homes on land that it owns.

10. NAMED SLY (two words) Moustached former *Match of the Day* and *Grandstand* presenter who launched a scathing attack on Gary Lineker in July, telling him to 'get on with the football'.

11. BAN HUMANITY JANENE (two words) Prime minister of Israel, who visited No. 10 in March.

12. CLUMPY ENCARTA (two words) British rock legend whose photography exhibition at the National Portrait Gallery highlighted his former band at the height of their popularity from 1963 to 1964.

13. NECK RUBE (two words) Veteran radio presenter who left Radio Two in March after thirty-one years.

14. ALGAE FINGER (two words) Right-wing British politician who hasn't had much to do since Brexit, but popped up in 2023 to complain that his bank accounts had been closed.

15. FT JINGLE SELF (two words) Sky Sports pundit who stepped down as host of *Gillette Soccer Saturday* in May after more than twenty-five years.

16. JOCK VINO VODKA (two words) Serbian tennis player who won his twenty-third grand slam at the 2023 French Open. Not a big fan of vaccines.

17. ARCHWAY FRAN (two words) London business district known for its massive buildings. In June HSBC announced that it was moving out of the area to a much smaller office, owing to the increase in hybrid working.

18. ENTITLE SERBIAN (two words) German theoretical physicist who was portrayed by Tom Conti in 2023's *Oppenheimer*.

19. ALLOW FIRES (two words) *EastEnders* character who returned to the show in 2023, played by Lucy Benjamin.

20. KILT TUGS VAM (two words) Austrian artist whose painting *Dame mit Fächer* (*Lady with a Fan*) sold for £85 million in May, a record for a work of art in a European auction.

21. DEGREE INWARDLY (two words) Member of eighties boyband Wham!, which was the subject of a 2023 Netflix documentary, released in June.

22. INSOLENT THEFTS (two words) Cartoon about a prehistoric family which originally aired in 1960. In 2023 it was announced that a reboot aimed at adult audiences was in the works.

23. EDEN FARMS (two words) Geordie singer-songwriter who played to one hundred thousand fans at St James's Park in June, and headlined the main stage at Leeds and Reading in August.

24. MULL GO (one word) *Lord of the Rings* character who received their own video game in 2023, which was so universally panned the production studio behind it stopped developing games altogether.

25. SKEET SNOB (two words) Swashbuckling cricketer who oversaw England's wildly inconsistent form in 2023. Likes a scrap.

ALL MIXED UP – ROUND 2 ANSWERS

1. Metallica

2. Tom Cruise

3. Stoke-on-Trent

4. *God of War: Ragnarök*

5. Karl Lagerfeld

6. France

7. *All Quiet on the Western Front*

8. Bud Light

9. John Lewis

10. Des Lynam

11. Benjamin Netanyahu

12. Paul McCartney

13. Ken Bruce

14. Nigel Farage

15. Jeff Stelling

16. Novak Djokovic

17. Canary Wharf

18. Albert Einstein

19. Lisa Fowler

20. Gustav Klimt

21. Andrew Ridgeley

22. *The Flintstones*

23. Sam Fender

24. Gollum

25. Ben Stokes

DOCTOR . . . WHO?

Doctor Who celebrated its sixtieth anniversary in 2023 (and managed to squeeze another year out of its tiresome, moral-lecturing franchise in the process) with *Sex Education*'s Ncuti Gatwa taking over the controls of the TARDIS. Can you name the actors that preceded him in the role of the Doctor from the dates and clues below?*

1. *(1963–1966)* The first actor to play the Doctor. His likeness has appeared in multiple *Doctor Who* episodes following his death in 1975, with Richard Hurndall and more recently David Bradley taking on the role of the original, grumpy iteration of the timelord.

2. *(1966–1969)* The first Doctor to use his now-famous sonic screwdriver – in 1968's *Fury from the Deep* – and the last to appear in black and white. Many of his episodes are now lost, as they're rubbish ... sorry, because in the 1960s it was common practice for the BBC to delete and reuse master tapes.

3. *(1970–1974)* Was known for spontaneously beating up enemies – the first Doctor to do so – with a martial arts style known as 'Venusian aikido'. Also played the title role in *Worzel Gummidge*.

---

* As there will no doubt be pedantic fans reading this, the answers only include the canonical numbered Doctors, and each actor only appears once, so no John Hurt, Peter Cushing or any of those contentious Brain of Morbius ones.

4. *(1974–1981)* The longest-serving Doctor, known for his trademark curly hair and long scarf. In more recent years he provided the voiceovers on *Little Britain* and is one of two Doctors to have hosted *Have I Got News for You.*

5. *(1982–1984)* At the time, was the youngest actor to have played the Doctor, and wore a questionable cricket-inspired outfit. Also enjoyed success as Tristan Farnon in *All Creatures Great and Small.*

6. *(1984–1986)* Arguably the most garishly dressed of all the Doctors, and one of three actors who had appeared in the show as a different character before getting the keys to the TARDIS. His tenure got off to a controversial start after he attempted to strangle his companion Peri moments after regenerating, which remains one of the most violent moments in the show's history. Admittedly, this is a tricky one, as absolutely no one was watching *Doctor Who* by this point.

7. *(1987–1989)* Any notion of subtlety was well and truly gone by the late eighties, and this version of the Doctor (the first to use a Scottish accent) had an umbrella with a question mark for a handle. Declining viewing figures resulted in the show being canned, until . . .

8. *(1996)* . . . the awful *Doctor Who: The Movie*, which was so badly received that the show would be shelved for another nine years. In the lead role this time was a well-known British actor who also starred opposite Richard E. Grant in cult classic *Withnail and I.*

9. *(2005)* The ninth Doctor lasted longer than the eighth, but not by much, quitting just one season after the series was resurrected by the BBC.

10. *(2005–2010)* Arguably the most popular Doctor of the modern era. Was accompanied by Billie Piper, Freema Agyeman and Catherine Tate, and spoke with an English accent despite being a proud Scot. Has taken on *Have I Got News for You* hosting duties on numerous occasions.

11. *(2010–2013)* The youngest actor to take on the role of the Doctor, aged just twenty-six at the time of casting. This incarnation occasionally wore a fez, and enjoyed the odd bowl of fish fingers and custard.

12. *(2013–2017)* Another Scottish actor, taking on a far more family-friendly role than the one he played in *The Thick of It*. Has also appeared on *Have I Got News for You*, as a panellist on Paul's team in 2006.

13. *(2018–2022)* The first woman to play the Doctor. Appeared alongside Bradley Walsh and an unbelievably wooden John Bishop.

Doctor . . . Who? – Answers

1. William Hartnell

2. Patrick Troughton

3. Jon Pertwee

4. Tom Baker

5. Peter Davison

6. Colin Baker

7. Sylvester McCoy

8. Paul McGann

9. Christopher Eccleston

10. David Tennant

11. Matt Smith

12. Peter Capaldi

13. Jodie Whittaker

Net zero 'still very much part of the government's plans' insisted Rishi Sunak – pictured here returning from Marks & Spencer:

HAVEN IS A PLACE ON EARTH

Only two things are certain in life: death, and wealthy people occasionally paying their taxes. Nadhim Zahawi found himself with some explaining to do early in the year when it was revealed he was investigated by HMRC while serving as chancellor under Boris Johnson. Can you place the following European tax havens on a map? This one shouldn't be too difficult if you know your geography or are Gary Barlow.

1. Bulgaria
2. Gibraltar
3. Czech Republic
4. Jersey
5. Liechtenstein
6. Montenegro
7. Switzerland
8. Malta
9. Denmark
10. Andorra

Haven is a Place on Earth – Answers

Stranger than Fiction – Round 2

Ten more groups of peculiar 2023 headlines, but can you work out which one is genuine?

1. A. Joe Pasquale impaled in freak moose antler incident in Skegness

   B. Orang-utan euthanised after Les Dennis falls into zoo enclosure

   C. Gemma Collins suffers concussion after walking into parked car

   D. Stephen Mulhern recovering after severe reaction to plum tomato

2. A. Texas woman seriously injured after hot-air balloon lands on top of her

   B. Texas woman seriously injured after falling head first into a festival toilet

   C. Texas woman seriously injured after hawk drops snake on her and both attack

   D. Texas woman seriously injured after microwaving her own head

3. A. Arrest warrant issued for man who forced owls to drink Dr Pepper

    B. Cops hunt man who 'offered boys a large amount of cash to kick him in the groin'

    C. Judge refuses bail for man who urinated on *Christ the Redeemer*'s feet

    D. Police defend use of pepper spray on man who refused to stop talking like Kermit the Frog

4. A. Pet tortoise discovered four months after being flushed down toilet

    B. Cat coaxed out of 'deepest mine shaft in Staffordshire' with packet of Scampi Fries

    C. Pet dog 'lucky to be alive' after eating nine Easter eggs

    D. Parrot missing for two days is rescued from a tree after being lured down with a bag of Wotsits

5. A. Glasgow man jailed for stealing 10,000 cans of Irn Bru

    B. Leeds man jailed for stealing 200,000 Cadbury's Creme Eggs

    C. Cardiff man jailed for stealing 500 packets of Mini Cheddars

    D. Belfast man jailed for stealing 50,000 cans of sweetcorn

6. A. Boris Johnson filmed throwing newts into his neighbour's garden

   B. Boris Johnson vows 'Newtopia' for amphibians ruining his swimming pool

   C. Boris Johnson offers £50 reward for pet newt missing since Friday

   D. Boris Johnson opens garden pond to public following discovery of rare newt

7. A. Huge sinkhole becomes tourist attraction in Manchester after sewer collapse

   B. Huge traffic cone becomes tourist attraction in Glasgow due to viral photo

   C. Huge seagull becomes tourist attraction in Brighton after eating a cat

   D. Huge sculpture of John Lennon becomes tourist attraction in New York due to uncanny resemblance to Harry Potter

8. A. Car-obsessed dad builds world's fastest Reliant Robin with top speed of 170mph

   B. IKEA-obsessed dad turns garage into miniature replica store, complete with tills and trolleys

   C. Erotica-obsessed dad turns house into sex museum with 10,000 vintage toys and dolls

   D. Cricket-obsessed dad pays £400 for Graham Gooch to attend his funeral

9. A. Handwritten will found in Aretha Franklin's couch ruled to be valid

   B. Court rules that Betty White's cat is entitled to $40 million inheritance

   C. Builders discover handwritten lyrics behind Whitney Houston's refrigerator

   D. Toilet that Elvis Presley died on sells at auction for $50,000

10. A. Pedro Pascal spotted in Northampton Pizza Hut wearing high heels and a fake beard

    B. Pedro Pascal's mum donates Range Rover to charity after winning it on a scratch card

    C. Pedro Pascal turns down *EastEnders* cameo due to 'irrational hatred of Shane Ritchie'

    D. Pedro Pascal visits UK art show dedicated to him, only to find he can't get in

Stranger than Fiction – Round 2 Answers

1. A – Joe Pasquale impaled in freak moose antler incident in Skegness (BBC News – 5 August). The comedian tripped and fell onto the antlers during a show, and only narrowly avoided stabbing himself in the stomach, injuring his leg instead. According to eyewitnesses, Joe Pasquale's high-pitched screaming suddenly stopped when he fell onto the antlers.

2. C – Texas woman seriously injured after hawk drops snake on her and both attack (*Evening Standard* – 9 August). A sixty-four-year-old woman from Texas was mowing her lawn when a hawk accidentally dropped a snake on her, before swooping down to reclaim its meal. In the wake of the incident, Republican politicians said the attackers could have been taken down by a good guy with a hawk and a snake.

3. B – Cops hunt man who 'offered boys a large amount of cash to kick him in the groin' (*Daily Star* – 31 July). Following reports of the bizarre incident, Cheshire police advised the public to be on the lookout for someone with a distinctive walk and a very high-pitched voice (but not Joe Pasquale, as he was accounted for and in the process of being removed from a moose antler).

4. D – Parrot missing for two days is rescued from a tree after being lured down with a bag of Wotsits (*Herald Sun* – 12 July). The parrot eventually came down when rescue workers brandished a bag of crispy snacks at it, suggesting it might have been called Russell.*

---

* Joke in the public domain since around 1948.

5. B – Leeds man jailed for stealing 200,000 Cadbury's Creme Eggs (Leeds Live – 20 July). A man who stole £31,000 worth of the chocolate eggs from an industrial unit in Telford was dubbed 'the Easter bunny' by police, which will undoubtedly strike fear into the hearts of the drug dealers and murderers he's locked up with.

6. B – Boris Johnson vows 'Newtopia' for amphibians ruining his swimming pool (Politico – 4 August). Boris Johnson's application to install an outdoor swimming pool at his Oxfordshire country manor was delayed due to the threat it would pose to great-crested newts. The former PM vowed to do everything he can to protect the newts, which historically means he's about to introduce sweeping cuts to their public services.

7. A – Huge sinkhole becomes tourist attraction in Manchester after sewer collapse (*Independent* – 18 July). The giant sinkhole – an open sewer full of wheelie bins – was declared Manchester's most picturesque location and awarded Grade II listed status.

8. C – Erotica-obsessed dad turns house into sex museum with 10,000 vintage toys and dolls (*Mirror* – 3 August). The fifty-six-year-old man from Vancouver, Canada estimates that he's spent more than $40,000 on his collection of sex toys. Visitors are welcome to view the collection, but are advised to be careful where they sit.

9. A – Handwritten will found in Aretha Franklin's couch ruled to be valid (*Forbes* – 11 July) After the will was found inside a couch that belonged to Aretha Franklin – who died in 2018 – solicitors said that it was genuine and they had no choice but to R-E-S-P-E-C-T her wishes.

10. D – Pedro Pascal visits UK art show dedicated to him, only to find he can't get in (CNN – 10 August). The *Mandalorian* and *Game of Thrones* actor happened upon an art exhibition dedicated to his likeness in Margate, only to find that the gallery was closed. Luckily there was a B&Q nearby, so he enjoyed roughly the same experience by walking through the mirror aisle.

NAME THAT CELEBRITY FEUD

One of the biggest (and certainly one of the least important) stories of 2023 was the reported behind-the-scenes falling out between *This Morning* presenters Holly Willoughby and Phillip Schofield, which culminated in the latter leaving the show in late May. Can you work out these famous celebrity feuds from the following initials and clues?

1. (PS, AG) American folk duo who have fallen out numerous times over the last five decades. Songs include 'Homeward Bound', 'Bridge Over Troubled Water' and 'The Boxer'.

2. (DT, ROD) American businessman and reality TV host who had a brief stint as president of the United States of America, and the comedian/actress he's feuded with for much of the last fifteen years, whose credits include *The Flintstones*, *A League of Their Own* and *Sleepless in Seattle*.

3. (DJ, VD) Musclebound stars of the Fast & Furious franchise, one of whom was previously a very successful professional wrestler.

4. (KW, TS) Two musicians who haven't seen eye-to-eye since one stormed the stage at the 2009 MTV Video Music Awards while the other was accepting an award.

5. (BD, JC) Two legendary Hollywood actresses who fell out on the set of *What Ever Happened to Baby Jane?* in 1962 and remained locked in a vicious feud for the rest of their lives.

6. (WS, CR) These two had an altercation at last year's Academy Awards, with one accusing the other of making disrespectful comments about his wife on several occasions.

7. (KC, SJP) *Sex and the City* actresses who reportedly fell out over money more than two decades ago and have remained on frosty terms ever since.

8. (LG, NG) Mancunian brothers who haven't been on speaking terms since their band broke up in 2009.

9. (AD, KB) Actors who didn't get along in real life despite appearing onscreen together as friendly droids C-3PO and R2-D2 in the first six *Star Wars* films.

10. (QEI, MQOS) English monarch and her cousin who some historians claim had an equal – if not greater – claim to the throne. Definitely one of the grisliest ends to any of the feuds on this list.

11. (BW, ML) Beach Boys bandmates whose decades-long feud was a far cry from their upbeat pop hits.

12. (M, JM) English rockers who haven't appeared onstage together since 1986. The former has some interesting views on immigration and Brexit.

13. (SJ, BG) Two titans of tech who started companies in the mid-1970s which are still competitors to this day.

14. (MC, HN) Considered to be two of the greatest chess players of all time, they had a huge falling out in 2022 when the actions of one, in abandoning a match against the other, were interpreted as a protest against cheating.

15. (MA, JF) Boxers who took part in the so-called 'Thrilla in Manilla' who made no secret of their intense dislike of each other outside of the ring.

16. (GP, MS) One makes candles that smell like vaginas and one went to prison. They've not been on each other's Christmas card lists since 2013, when the latter took aim at the former's new-age healthcare brand.

17. (RW, DG) British rockers who haven't performed together since Live 8 in 2005, and are unlikely to do so again following another huge argument in February, with the latter's spouse accusing the former of antisemitism, and the former responding by threatening legal action.

18. (EJ, M) Two legendary singers who have traded barbs ever since one branded the other's Bond theme as the worst in the franchise.

19. (TH, NK) Ice skaters whose rivalry spiralled out of control at the 1994 US Figure Skating Championships when one was assaulted and had to withdraw.

20. (BS, TS) Two of the most influential rappers of all time, who feuded throughout their short careers and died within six months of each other in similar circumstances.

Name that Celebrity Feud – Answers

1. Paul Simon and Art Garfunkel

2. Donald Trump and Rosie O'Donnell

3. Dwayne Johnson and Vin Diesel

4. Kanye West and Taylor Swift

5. Bette Davis and Joan Crawford

6. Will Smith and Chris Rock

7. Kim Cattrall and Sarah Jessica Parker

8. Liam Gallagher and Noel Gallagher

9. Anthony Daniels and Kenny Baker

10. Queen Elizabeth I and Mary, Queen of Scots

11. Brian Wilson and Mike Love

12. Morrissey and Johnny Marr

13. Steve Jobs and Bill Gates

14. Magnus Carlsen and Hans Niemann

15. Muhammad Ali and Joe Frazier

16. Gwyneth Paltrow and Martha Stewart

17. Roger Waters and David Gilmour

18. Elton John and Madonna

19. Tonya Harding and Nancy Kerrigan

20. Biggie Smalls and Tupac Shakur

YOU'RE GROUNDED!

At the end of August, an air traffic control issue caused the UK's worst period of travel disruption since that Icelandic volcano with the incredibly long name erupted in 2010. Can you identify the following major airports from their three-digit identification codes?

1. LHR
2. BER
3. GIB
4. LAX
5. HAV
6. CAI
7. LXR
8. BUE
9. SFO
10. CUN
11. CAS
12. LTN
13. CHI
14. IBZ
15. DBV

You're Grounded! – Answers

1. LHR – London Heathrow

2. BER – Berlin

3. GIB – Gibraltar

4. LAX – Los Angeles International

5. HAV – Havana

6. CAI – Cairo

7. LXR – Luxor

8. BUE – Buenos Aires

9. SFO – San Francisco

10. CUN – Cancún

11. CAS – Casablanca

12. LTN – Luton

13. CHI – Chicago

14. IBZ – Ibiza

15. DBV – Dubrovnik

FIND THE MPS' SURNAMES HIDDEN WITHIN THESE INCREASINGLY CONTRIVED SENTENCES

Below are twenty sentences that – at first glance – are absolute gibberish. Hidden within them, however, are the surnames of twenty prominent MPs who served in 2023. How many can you find? We'll start with an easy one . . .

1. It would take a braver man than me to stand up to those aggressive bullies.
2. Would I let her borrow my brand-new Vauxhall Zafira? Absolutely!
3. Since Bert was extremely self-conscious about his shortest arm, Ernie offered to balance it out by sawing three inches off the longer one.
4. The Manchester City team bus had arrived two hours late, and as a result Pep ate lunch much later than usual.
5. It was clear nobody knew Gary and Brenda were stuck in the sexual health clinic, or by now someone would have come looking for them.
6. John's only hope now was that his loan shark agreed to write off his debt, but given how much he owed, that was highly unlikely.
7. The children's birthday party was absolute Bedlam. My ears would be ringing for a week!

8. Despite Lucy's best efforts to find an explanation for her extremely large, pink wart, England's best dermatologists had yet to offer any sort of rational explanation.

9. Peter glanced anxiously at his mobile. Although his friends were clearly in a rush, apps were still updating and if his phone wasn't ready, then neither was he.

10. The idea of a day out at what the local tourist brochure described as a 'prefab bottle factory' didn't sound particularly exciting.

11. The oncoming mercenaries charged while their opponents were blinded by the sun, AK-47s at the ready, some of which had been turned into makeshift bayonets.

12. Were three vests too many? Simon looked out of the window and the snow was coming down heavier than ever. Perhaps an extra one couldn't hurt.

13. The goal was nodded in by Wilfried Zaha with ninety-three minutes on the clock. But was it offside?

14. The security breach at the Star Trek convention threw the event into total disarray. Nerds and geeks of all shapes and sizes clambered over the fence in the hope of meeting William Shatner.

15. Despite Dmitri's lifelong dream to own a Portuguese terrapin, Chernobyl had made local water sources too radioactive, so he got a dog instead.

16. The film crew watched in awe as the brown and yellow Peruvian tree frog walked right in front of the camera.

17. Jim checked the chicken coop in disbelief. Somehow, he'd returned from the farmers' market with fewer chickens than cockerels for the second time in a month.

18. The supposed 'cabaret evening' consisted of an awful ventriloquist, an out-of-tune opera singer and an overweight Russell Crowe impersonator.

19. Squeezing six people into the car surely wouldn't do any harm, and besides, they were only driving three miles up the road. What's the worst that could happen?

20. Rupert could scarcely believe he was driving down the longest street in Gillingham.

Find the MPs' Surnames Hidden Within these Increasingly Contrived Sentences – Answers

1. It would take a **BRAVER MAN** than me to stand up to those aggressive bodybuilders.

2. Would I let her borrow my brand-new Vauxhall ZafiRA? ABsolutely!

3. Since Bert was extremely self-conscious about his short-eST ARM, ERnie offered to balance it out by sawing three inches off the longer one.

4. The Manchester City team bus had arrived two hours late, and as a result PeP ATE Lunch much later than usual.

5. It was clear nobody knew Gary and Brenda were stuck in the sexual health cliniC, **OR BY** Now someone would have come looking for them.

6. **JOHN'S ON**ly hope now was that his loan shark agreed to write off his debt, but given how much he owed, that was highly unlikely.

7. The children's birthday party was absolute BedLAM. **MY** ears would be ringing for a week!

8. Despite Lucy's best efforts to find an explanation for her extremely large, pinK WART, ENGland's best dermatologists had yet to offer any sort of rational explanation.

9. Peter glanced anxiously at his mobile. Although his friends were clearly in a ruSH, APPS were still updating and if his phone wasn't ready, then neither was he.

10. The idea of a day out at what the local tourist brochure described as a 'prefAB BOTTle factory' didn't sound particularly exciting.

11. The oncoming mercenaries charged while their opponents were blinded by the SUN, AK-47s at the ready, some of which had been turned into makeshift bayonets.

12. Were thREE VESts too many? Simon looked out of the window and the snow was coming down heavier than ever. Perhaps an extra one couldn't hurt.

13. The goal was nodded in by Wilfried ZAHA WIth ninety-three minutes on the clock. But was it offside?

14. The security breach at the Star Trek convention threw the event into total disarRAY. NERds and geeks of all shapes and sizes clambered over the fence in the hope of meeting William Shatner.

15. Despite Dmitri's lifelong dream to own a Portuguese terraPIN, CHERnobyl had made local water sources too radioactive, so he got a dog instead.

16. The film crew watched in awe as the browN AND Yellow Peruvian tree frog walked right in front of the camera.

17. Jim checked the chicken coop in disbelief. Somehow, he'd returned from the farmers' market with fewer chickens tHAN COCKerels for the second time in a month.

18. The supposed 'cabaret evening' consisted of an awful ventriloquist, an out-of-tune opera singer and an over-weighT RUSSell Crowe impersonator.

19. Squeezing six people into the car surely wouldn't do any HARM, ANd besides, they were only driving three miles up the road. What's the worst that could happen?

20. Rupert could scarcely believe he was driving down the longest STREET IN Gillingham.

Following the release of the partygate report, a
photograph from an aide's phone revealed how staff
managed to discreetly sneak bottles of booze into No. 10:

MISSING WORDS – ROUND 2

Ten more incomplete headlines to have a crack at.

1. Charles Bronson has never _____ and would need practical support if released, expert reveals
   Sky News – 8 March

   A. Used a cash machine
   B. Driven a car
   C. Changed a lightbulb
   D. Put the bins out

2. _____ shares his horror over learning 'naked lookalike' is making £1k a day on OnlyFans
   Evening Standard – 17 March

   A. Eamonn Holmes
   B. Alan Titchmarsh
   C. Adrian Chiles
   D. Gregg Wallace

3. Scientists slam 'cruel' plans for world's first
_____ after blueprints leaked

EuroNews – 16 March

 A. Cockfighting arena

 B. Badger guillotine

 C. Octopus farm

 D. Chimpanzee Amazon warehouse

4. Woman, 91, loses account and pension after Barclays

_____

Guardian – 7 March

 A. Transfers them to a Nigerian 'prince'

 B. Accidentally sells her identity

 C. Deletes her postcode from its system

 D. Declares her dead

5. Roman Kemp mortified as he realises he accidentally
ate _____ worth £10,000

Mirror – 20 March

 A. Truffle

 B. Creme Egg

 C. Pork scratching

 D. Sushi

6. Smelling _____ could reduce social anxiety, suggests study
   Metro – 27 March

   A. Your partner's feet
   B. Fresh manure
   C. Skunks
   D. Other people's sweat

7. Woman mistaken for _____ 'fended off advances' while searching for neglected cat
   Daily Star – 24 March

   A. Randy dogger
   B. Beast of Bodmin
   C. Ulrika Jonsson
   D. Greg Davies

8. Colombia is being forced to spend $3.5 million moving Pablo Escobar's _____
   Yahoo! Finance – 30 March

   A. Grave
   B. Childhood home
   C. Hippos
   D. Car collection

9. Man so annoyed with potholes he's filling them with
   _____ to get them fixed
   Mirror – 30 March

    A. Jelly

    B. Angel Delight

    C. Curry powder

    D. Pot Noodles

10. Japanese firm starts selling _____ meat from vending
    machines with £13 packs of wild caught produce
    already proving popular
    Daily Mail – 3 April

    A. Bear

    B. Rat

    C. Spider

    D. Badger

Missing Words – Round 2 Answers

1. A – Charles Bronson has never **used a cash machine** and would need practical support if released, expert reveals. A parole hearing in March heard that Charles Bronson would struggle with freedom due to a lack of experience with everyday activities like using a cash machine, although Rishi Sunak suffers the same limitations and he's done all right for himself.

2. C – **Adrian Chiles** shares his horror over learning 'naked lookalike' is making £1k a day on OnlyFans, which is far more than the real thing makes for writing columns about there being too many varieties of hot cross bun on the *Guardian* website.

3. C – Scientists slam 'cruel' plans for world's first **octopus farm** after blueprints leaked. Animal rights activists were outraged at plans for the Canary Islands-based octopus farm, as despite the extra limbs they can only harvest crops marginally faster than humans.

4. D – Woman, 91, loses account and pension after Barclays **declares her dead**. The woman was forced to travel twenty-three miles to her nearest branch after her pension was returned to the DWP, who argued that just because someone is ninety-one and dead is no excuse to not be working.

5. B – Roman Kemp mortified as he realises he accidentally ate **Creme Egg** worth £10,000. Radio presenter Kemp – son of Spandau Ballet's Martin – tweeted a photograph of a half-milk/half-white chocolate Creme Egg after he'd eaten it, only to find out that it was worth £10,000 due to a contest being

run by Cadbury's. Then again, at 2023 prices, ten grand would only cover about six more Creme Eggs anyway.

6. D – Smelling **other people's sweat** could reduce social anxiety, suggests study. Scientists in Sweden suggested that sniffing a sweaty person could be useful in therapy for social anxiety. Not much use to Sarah Ferguson in couples counselling then.

7. A – Woman mistaken for **randy dogger** 'fended off advances' while searching for neglected cat. A twenty-nine-year-old woman from Bolton was besieged by horny weirdos while searching a notorious dogging hotspot for a missing cat, and asking them if they'd seen her pussy certainly didn't help. (Joke courtesy of *Are You Being Served?* circa 1972.)

8. C – Colombia is being forced to spend $3.5 million moving Pablo Escobar's **hippos**. Seventy of the notorious drug lord's pet hippos were moved to sanctuaries early in 2023, due to tourists gathering them into groups of four and making them compete for plastic balls.

9. D – Man so annoyed with potholes he's filling them with **Pot Noodles** to get them fixed. A man from Oxfordshire known as 'Mr Pothole' made headlines in 2023 for filling them with the instant snacks to bring them to the attention of his local council, although if they're small enough to be filled by a single Pot Noodle then he probably doesn't know how good he's got it. It's also not known whether he added the little sachet of soy sauce.

10. A – Japanese firm starts selling **bear** meat from vending machines with £13 packs of wild caught produce already proving popular. Although considered a delicacy in Japan, you need to be careful with bear meat, as the lesser-quality stuff can be a bit grizzly.

Real or Fake Coronation Tradition?

If we learned anything from King Charles's coronation (other than the fact Prince Andrew can cross the threshold into places of worship without bursting into flames) it's that royal ceremonial events are extremely outdated and impossibly pretentious. Can you separate the genuine coronation traditions below from the ones that are completely made up?

1. The Earl of Loudoun presents the Golden Spurs and holds them in a close proximity to the sovereign's feet.

2. A pheasant selected by the head groundskeeper of Westminster Abbey is slaughtered, and a single feather is sent to every Commonwealth nation twenty-one days before the coronation, which acts as an invitation to the ceremony.

3. The royal consort cannot see the monarch until senior military leaders separately confirm that there are no plots on either of their lives.

4. After the sovereign has sworn their oath, they will not take the throne on their own steam, but must be lifted into it by members of the congregation.

5. The sovereign will be anointed behind a golden canopy, so that the moment is witnessed only by the Archbishop of Canterbury.

6. There is a twenty-one-gun salute known as 'the divine whispering' which takes place during the ceremony, and actually consists of twenty-two firings; the extra one represents the deceased monarch who is being succeeded.

7. One of England's oldest laws states that a minimum of three hymns must be sung in Latin during the coronation ceremony. This has been honoured at every ceremony since Henry III.

8. The Stone of Destiny makes its way from Scotland to a specially designed hollow beneath the coronation chair, where it will remain until the ceremony is over.

9. During the service, a member of the congregation will offer one hundred silver shillings in exchange for the Sword of Offering.

10. Exactly one hundred days after the coronation, the monarch takes part in a private ceremony where they are anointed with the blood of a raven. Until the sixteenth century this was the official start point of a monarch's reign.

REAL OR FAKE CORONATION TRADITION? – ANSWERS

Real

1. The Earl of Loudoun presents the Golden Spurs and holds them in a close proximity to the sovereign's feet.

4. After the sovereign has sworn their oath, they will not take the throne on their own steam, but must be lifted into it by members of the congregation.

5. The sovereign will be anointed behind a golden canopy, so that the moment is witnessed only by the Archbishop of Canterbury.

8. The Stone of Destiny makes its way from Scotland to a specially designed hollow beneath the coronation chair, where it will remain until the ceremony is over.

9. During the service, a member of the congregation will offer one hundred silver shillings in exchange for the Sword of Offering.

Fake

2. A pheasant selected by the head groundskeeper of Westminster Abbey is slaughtered, and a single feather is sent to every Commonwealth nation twenty-one days before the coronation, which acts as an invitation to the ceremony.

3. The royal consort cannot see the monarch until senior military leaders separately confirm that there are no plots on either of their lives.

6. There is a twenty-one-gun salute known as 'the divine whispering' which takes place during the ceremony, and actually consists of twenty-two firings; the extra one represents the deceased monarch who is being succeeded.

7. One of England's oldest laws states that a minimum of three hymns must be sung in Latin during the coronation ceremony. This has been honoured at every ceremony since Henry III.

10. Exactly one hundred days after the coronation, the monarch takes part in a private ceremony where they are anointed with the blood of a raven. Until the sixteenth century this was the official start point of a monarch's reign.

PRACTICE SHOTS

On 6 June, the PGA Tour merged with LIV Golf, which came as a bit of a surprise as the two companies had spent much of the previous year locked in antitrust lawsuits. LIV is backed by Saudi Arabia, so the answers to this crossword – in the true spirit of golf – are all countries with similarly indefensible human rights records.

Across

2. Asian country with a leader that looks a bit like Winnie the Pooh. Despite not providing official figures, it is widely believed to have the highest rate of capital punishment of any country in the world, with Amnesty International estimating that at least one thousand people were executed in 2022 alone. (5)

5. Not somewhere you'd go if you wanted to buy western goods post 2022. In the north you'd be very cold, whereas in the south you'd be drafted into the military, whether you like it or not ... (6)

8. Known as Burma until 1989. Things have been especially grim here since a military coup in 2021, which resulted in the arrest and deposition of State Counsellor Aung San Suu Kyi. (7)

9. Large country located between Iraq and Afghanistan, and separated from Saudi Arabia by the Persian Gulf. Favours its own solar calendar over lunar and Gregorian models. Oh, and Amnesty International estimates that at least 576 people were executed here in 2022. (4)

Down

1. Middle Eastern country that was ranked sixth worst on the 2023 Press Freedom Index. Home to both the oldest library and the oldest capital city in the world. (5)

3. Secretive dictatorship with a penchant for firing rubbish missiles into the sea, and which – according to Amnesty International – has around two hundred thousand prisoners detained in camps dedicated to political crimes. In 2018, Donald Trump became the first sitting US president to visit here. (5,5)

4. Was bombed by the UK in 2011, at a reported cost of £1 billion. It is home to Africa's largest proven oil reserves, and in April 2023 the United Nations Human Rights Council heard that there were reasonable grounds to believe that citizens and migrants have been victims of crimes against humanity. (5)

6. West Asian country that has been in a state of civil war since 2011. Men can divorce women at will, whereas women need to provide justification for ending their marriage, and the country also has one of the worst child marriage records in the world. No other country in the world begins with the same letter. (5)

7. Nowadays it is the country most closely associated with piracy. It has the longest coastline of any African nation, and homosexual acts are punishable with prison terms of up to three years. (7)

Practice Shots – Solution

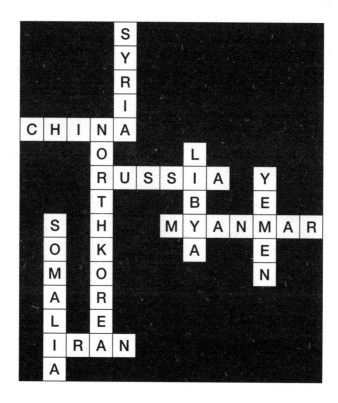

ALL MIXED UP: G20 EDITION

The 2023 G20 summit was the first ever to be held in India – in New Delhi – as well as South Asia, providing world leaders with an exciting new venue to announce policies they had no plans whatsoever of implementing. Can you name all of the G20 members from the anagrams below? To mix things up a bit (so to speak) clues in this round are replaced with each member's flag, but you might find it useful to know the answers are also in alphabetical order . . .

1. GREATNINA

2. LARIATUSA

3. LIZRAB

4. AAADNC

5. AHINC

6. UNIRONEUPNOEA

7. CANERF

8. NEARGYM

9. DIANI

10. IONSENDAI

11. LAITY

12. ANAPJ

13. ECOMIX

14. SARIUS

15. AURABASIDIA

16. AORTAFICHUS

17. ATREUSHOOK

18. RETYUK

19. DEMIGODUNKNIT

20. AUSTINDETEST

All Mixed Up: G20 Edition – Answers

1. Argentina

2. Australia

3. Brazil

4. Canada

5. China

6. European Union

7. France

8. Germany

9. India

10. Indonesia

11. Italy

12. Japan

13. Mexico

14. Russia

15. Saudi Arabia

16. South Africa

17. South Korea

18. Turkey

19. United Kingdom

20. United States

Following a strong performance by the Lib Dems at the 2023 local elections, Ed Davey's family said enough is enough and stepped in after he tried to fire himself out of a blue cannon:

FURTHER MATHS WITH RISHI SUNAK

On 4 January, Rishi Sunak – in his first speech of the year – announced plans to make mathematics mandatory for all pupils up to the age of eighteen. Like most modern government pledges, it fell by the wayside almost immediately, but here's what a Rishi Sunak maths test might have looked like had he followed through with it.

1. If Richard arranges a loan of £800,000 for Boris, how much will Boris have to pay back if interest is fixed at 20 per cent?

2. If it takes six Labour MPs four weeks to come up with three policies, how long would it take twenty-four Labour MPs to come up with six policies?

3. Vladimir has ninety-six tanks. If forty-eight are captured by Ukrainian farmers, how many does he have left?

4. On Monday, Harry and Meghan receive three column inches. On Tuesday they kick off about something or other and receive six column inches. If the column inches continue to double every day, how many will they receive on Sunday?

5. If a train is due to leave Manchester Piccadilly at 9.45 a.m. on Tuesday but is delayed by six hours and thirty-five minutes, followed by a twenty-four-hour strike, when will it leave?

6. If Keir purges fifteen Corbynites in January, twenty-eight in February and twelve in March, how many has he purged in total?

7. If Grant, Sebastian, Corrine and Michael each have four aliases, each of which themselves have three aliases, how many aliases are there in total?

8. Roald writes a children's book with a total of forty-five thousand words. If his publishers cut 20 per cent of them for being too offensive, how many words remain?

9. If Ed orders a giant blue clock on Thursday, and it takes nineteen days to arrive, on which day of the week will it be delivered?

10. Suella sets an ambitious target of deporting five thousand people, but only achieves 2 per cent of this. How many people are deported?

FURTHER MATHS WITH RISHI SUNAK – ANSWERS

1. Boris will pay back £960,000.

2. It would take two weeks.

3. Vladimir will be left with forty-eight tanks.

4. Harry and Meghan will receive 192 column inches on Sunday.

5. The train will leave on Wednesday at 4.20 p.m.

6. Keir has purged fifty-five Corbynites.

7. There are sixty-four aliases.

8. Thirty-six thousand words remain in Roald's book.

9. The giant blue clock will arrive on a Tuesday.

10. One hundred people are deported.

SPOT THE WMD

2023 marked the twentieth anniversary of the invasion of Iraq, and as such, our good friends Tony and Alastair claim that there are weapons of mass destruction hidden in this photograph of Baghdad. How many can you find?

Spot the WMD – Answers

As the book goes to print Tony and Alastair have yet to provide the answers, but keep looking and there will hopefully be an update on this in *Have I Got News for You: The Quiz of 2024.*

WHAT'S IN A NAME?

On 17 April, Wales's Brecon Beacons changed its name to the far catchier Bannau Brycheiniog in both Welsh and English. Below are ten other places that used to be known as something else, but can you match them to (in some cases, one of) their previous names?

1.	Ho Chi Minh City	A.	New Amsterdam
2.	Mumbai	B.	Leningrad
3.	Toronto	C.	Siam
4.	Iran	D.	Ceylon
5.	Thailand	E.	Swaziland
6.	New York	F.	York
7.	Sri Lanka	G.	Saigon
8.	Saint Petersburg	H.	Bombay
9.	Eswatini	I.	Persia
10.	Zimbabwe	J.	Rhodesia

WHAT'S IN A NAME? – ANSWERS

1. G – Ho Chi Minh City – Saigon (changed name in 1976)

2. H – Mumbai – Bombay (1995)

3. F – Toronto – York (1834)

4. I – Iran – Persia (1935)

5. C – Thailand – Siam (1939)

6. A – New York – New Amsterdam (1664)

7. D – Sri Lanka – Ceylon (1972)

8. B – Saint Petersburg – Leningrad (1991)

9. E – Eswatini – Swaziland (2018)

10. J – Zimbabwe – Rhodesia (1980)

Afghan Hound or Michael Fabricant?

One's shaggy, obedient, and shouldn't be let off its lead in public, the other is an Afghan hound. Can you find the Michael Fabricants hidden among the stock images of dogs?

1.

2.

3.

4.

5.

6.

Afghan Hound or Michael Fabricant? – Answers

1.

2.

3.

4.

5.

6.

LOCATION, LOCATION, LOCATION

Below is a list of ten famous locations from around the world (and beyond), but can you match them up with the reason they made headlines in 2023?

1. The Eiffel Tower
2. BBC Maida Vale Studios
3. *Christ the Redeemer*
4. Royal Yacht *Britannia*
5. The moon
6. Pompeii
7. Harrods
8. The Great Pyramid of Giza
9. The Taj Mahal
10. Mount Everest

A. Was struck by an out-of-control Russian craft on 19 August.
B. Permits for foreigners to climb to the top of this location rose from $11,000 to $15,000 in 2023.
C. Archaeologists announced the discovery of a nine-metre-long tunnel in March, thought to lead to the tomb of an ancient king.
D. Reported profits of £135.8 million for the year ending 28 January.

E. Two heavily intoxicated American tourists were handed over to police after getting trapped and spending the night here in August.

F. Was named best UK attraction in the 2023 Tripadvisor Travellers' Choice Awards

G. Was sold to a partnership consisting of Hans Zimmer and three film producers in August.

H. Climate activists projected the Doomsday Clock onto this towering erection in June.

I. Archaeologists uncovered a 2,000-year-old fresco of what they believe to be a 'pizza-style dish' during a dig here in June.

J. Flood waters reached the walls of this famous site in July for the first time since 1978.

LOCATION, LOCATION, LOCATION – ANSWERS

1. E. Eiffel Tower – Two heavily intoxicated American tourists were handed over to police after getting trapped and spending the night here in August.

2. G. BBC Maida Vale Studios – Was sold to a partnership consisting of Hans Zimmer and three film producers in August.

3. H. *Christ the Redeemer* – Climate activists projected the Doomsday Clock onto this towering erection in June.

4. F. Royal Yacht *Britannia* – Was named best UK attraction in the 2023 Tripadvisor Travellers' Choice Awards

5. A. The moon – Was struck by an out-of-control Russian craft on 19 August.

6. I. Pompeii – Archaeologists uncovered a 2,000-year-old fresco of what they believe to be a 'pizza style dish' during a dig here in June.

7. D. Harrods – Reported profits of £135.8 million for the year ending 28 January.

8. C. Great Pyramid of Giza – Archaeologists announced the discovery of a nine-metre-long tunnel in March, thought to lead to the tomb of an ancient king.

9. J. The Taj Mahal – Flood waters reached the walls of this famous site in July for the first time since 1978.

10. B. Mount Everest – Permits for foreigners to climb to the top of this location rose from $11,000 to $15,000 in 2023.

The 2023 Air Guitar World Championships
descended into chaos after one entrant tore up
the rule book and played a synthesiser:

HEROES AND VILLAINS

Superhero films continued to be forced down everyone's throats in 2023, probably because there are few real-life heroes to look up to. Given the widely terrible reviews of these films and their non-existent plots, we've come up with some loglines below to inspire the studios for their next sequels – a fictional superhero pitted against a real-life villain (or at least person of questionable moral fortitude). Can you figure out who's who?

1. Man whose weakness is getting trapped under a glass heads north across the demilitarised zone to take out a dictator with a terrible haircut.

2. Scientist with a short fuse and a habit of changing colour hides in an oversized box in order to launch a surprise attack on a bald-headed retail entrepreneur.

3. Woman puts her nine lives to the test in a high-stakes battle at Four Seasons Total Landscaping.

4. Africa's most powerful hero heads back in time to Prohibition-era New York to take out the city's most notorious crime boss.

5. Man with a patriotic shield risks another cold war after setting his sights on one of Europe's most unhinged leaders.

6. Woman with magic lasso takes on one of the universe's most irritating media personalities during the recording of a *Gavin and Stacey* Christmas special.

7. Man who can see through walls attempts to prevent an explosion on 5 November 1605.

8. Man who sleeps upside-down in a loft tries to avoid becoming a human kebab in fifteenth-century Romania.

9. Norse god of thunder arrives in seventeenth-century England tasked with saving Christmas.

10. Anthropomorphic teddy bear with superpowers sneaks into a German bunker on 30 April 1945.

Heroes and Villains – Answers

1. Spider-Man vs Kim Jong-un

2. The Incredible Hulk vs Jeff Bezos

3. Catwoman vs Rudy Giuliani

4. Black Panther vs Al Capone

5. Captain America vs Vladimir Putin

6. Wonder Woman vs James Corden

7. Superman vs Guy Fawkes

8. Batman vs Vlad the Impaler

9. Thor vs Oliver Cromwell

10. SuperTed vs Adolf Hitler

ROYAL RUMBLE

The first half of 2023 was fairly eventful for the royal family, with the release of Prince Harry's memoir, *Spare*, the build-up to the coronation, and Prince Andrew, well … existing. Here are ten questions about a busy few months for the newly installed King Charles.

1. Sales of Elizabeth Arden Eight Hour Cream increased following the release of *Spare* due to the revelation that Harry had used it to treat what?

    A. A jellyfish sting

    B. Frostbite

    C. Scabies

    D. Mosquito bites

2. The book also alleged that while Harry was growing up, his father travelled everywhere with a 'pitiful' what?

    A. Teapot

    B. Handkerchief

    C. Blanket

    D. Teddy bear

3. Which US comedy show took aim at the Sussexes with an episode titled 'The Worldwide Privacy Tour'?

    A. *Family Guy*
    B. *The Simpsons*
    C. *South Park*
    D. *Bob's Burgers*

4. In February it emerged that Prince Andrew was facing pressure to downsize from Windsor's Royal Lodge mansion to Harry and Meghan's old house, which only has a meagre ten bedrooms. What is the residence called?

    A. Wren House
    B. Adelaide Cottage
    C. Frogmore Cottage
    D. Highgrove House

5. As Prince Andrew's privileges continued to be stripped back in March, King Charles reportedly informed him that he would no longer foot the bill – allegedly £32,000 a year – for what?

    A. Private tennis lessons
    B. A live-in yoga instructor
    C. His energy bills
    D. His expensive taste in wine

6. What title was given to Prince Edward to mark his fifty-ninth birthday on 10 March?

    A. Duke of Edinburgh

    B. Baron of Rothesay

    C. Earl of Wessex

    D. Marquess of Chichester

7. Two months prior to Charles's coronation, what was revealed about the sacred oil that would be used to anoint him?

    A. It contained the blood of three different animals

    B. It was vegan

    C. It was the same mixture used to anoint Henry VIII

    D. The capsule used to contain it had been looted from Nazi Germany

8. A song by which band was removed from the official coronation playlist after they were criticised for their anti-royal views?

    A. Elbow

    B. The Proclaimers

    C. Jedward

    D. Duran Duran

9. How did chocolate company Cadbury celebrate the coronation?

    A. With a chocolate fondue party at Balmoral

    B. They reverted the design of some wrappers to how they looked in 1953

    C. By making a chocolate version of King Charles's coronation crown

    D. By having Prince Andrew burst out of a giant tub of Roses

10. Mere days before the ceremony, the reputation of the official coronation quiche was thrown into question when French experts claimed it was actually a what?

    A. Pie

    B. Cake

    C. Pudding

    D. Tart

Royal Rumble – Answers

1. B – Harry revealed that he used the cream on his penis when it became frostbitten during a trip to the North Pole in 2011. It's never really explained why his penis and only his penis became frostbitten, but 'crotchless SS uniform' is the most popular theory.

2. D – The book claimed that Prince (now King) Charles always travelled with a threadbare teddy bear, which in recent years has been replaced with a Meghan Markle voodoo doll.

3. C – It was *South Park*. Although the Sussexes aren't explicitly named in the episode, it features a British prince and his 'attention-seeking' wife, who embark on a worldwide tour demanding people respect their privacy. It's not the first time *South Park* has caused outrage with a storyline about the royal family, as a 2007 episode about terrorists placing a bomb in Hillary Clinton's stomach (yes, really) culminates with Queen Elizabeth II committing suicide by shooting herself in the head.

4. C – Frogmore Cottage was Harry and Meghan's UK residence, until they were politely asked to vacate it in early 2023. Early reports suggested that Prince Andrew was resisting the move to Frogmore Cottage, until King Charles swiftly resolved the situation with some rope and a cattle prod.

5. B – Prince Andrew's use of a live-in yoga instructor raised a lot of questions, not least over how recruiters had convinced a yoga instructor to move in with Prince Andrew for just thirty-two grand.

6. A – King Charles gave his brother the title of Duke of Edinburgh for his birthday, after Edward successfully completed a twenty-mile hike in the Peak District followed by three nights in a tent eating beans with a straw.

7. B – The oil used to anoint Charles was vegan friendly, unlike the oil used for his mum's coronation, which contained ingredients taken from a sperm whale, a musk deer and a civet cat. The move was welcomed by the massive numbers of royalist vegans, thought to be anywhere between three and four people.

8. B – The Proclaimers' song 'I'm Gonna Be (500 Miles)' was pulled from King Charles's official coronation playlist due to the band's alleged anti-royal views, coming as disappointing news to the handful of psychopaths who would willingly listen to a King Charles-themed playlist.

9. C – Cadbury unveiled an edible replica of King Charles's coronation crown, which – in keeping with tradition – included a Wispa Gold that was stolen from India in the nineteenth century.

10. D – The royal coronation quiche was in fact a 'banal tart' according to the grand master of the Brotherhood of the Quiche Lorraine (which, despite sounding like something from Monty Python, is a real organisation). King Charles quickly hit back at the 'banal tart' accusation, before realising they weren't talking about Camilla.

GENERAL KNOWLEDGE — ROUND 3

Another round of miscellaneous questions from 2023 . . .

1. What immortal words did Holly Willoughby utter when she returned to *This Morning* for the first time since Phillip Schofield's departure on 5 June?

   A. Right, deep breath. Firstly, are you OK? I hope so

   B. Phil might have gone, but his spirit lives on

   C. Today I'm speaking to a man who claims to own a haunted car

   D. Thank god for that. I thought he'd never leave

2. During the build-up to the FA Cup replay between Liverpool and Wolves on 17 January, Gary Lineker was speaking to Danny Murphy and Alan Shearer when what happened?

   A. A dog ran through the studio

   B. Loud sex sounds began playing

   C. Fans started an offensive chant about Gary Lineker

   D. One of them said something interesting

3. Which government minister completed the 2023 London Marathon?

    A. Steve Barclay

    B. Suella Braverman

    C. Jeremy Hunt

    D. Oliver Dowden

4. On 6 July, Keir Starmer outlined Labour's education plans at an event in Kent while surrounded by local students. What unexpectedly happened midway through his speech?

    A. One of the students fainted

    B. A wasp caused one of the students to scream

    C. A fire alarm set off the venue's sprinklers

    D. Two of the students launched a climate protest

5. Who did Andy Murray invite to sit in the royal box at Wimbledon to watch his first-round match against Ryan Peniston?

    A. David Tennant

    B. Rafael Nadal

    C. Nicola Sturgeon

    D. Nazanin Zaghari-Ratcliffe

6. A clip of Hugh Grant being interviewed by Ashley Graham on the Oscars red carpet went viral due to the *Notting Hill* actor's short, grumpy answers. Why was he particularly annoyed when she asked him about his appearance in *Glass Onion: A Knives Out Mystery*?

    A. He wasn't in the film
    B. He only had a brief cameo
    C. He'd publicly denounced the director
    D. She was supposed to ask him about a different film

7. Which 2023 film was banned in Vietnam due to its depiction of the South China Sea?

    A. *Mission: Impossible – Dead Reckoning Part One*
    B. *Barbie*
    C. *Guardians of the Galaxy Vol. 3*
    D. *The Super Mario Bros. Movie*

8. 8. In March, the editor-in-chief of German magazine *Die Aktuelle* was relieved of their duties following the publication of an AI-generated interview with which sporting legend?

    A. Pelé
    B. Michael Schumacher
    C. Muhammad Ali
    D. Seve Ballesteros

9. Just days before Glastonbury 2023, organisers banned the screening of a film about which British politician, which was due to take place at the festival?

    A. Jeremy Corbyn

    B. Caroline Lucas

    C. Tony Blair

    D. Nigel Farage

10. In July a tourist from England found himself in hot water after carving his name into a wall at which historic location?

    A. The Leaning Tower of Pisa

    B. Pompeii

    C. The Sistine Chapel

    D. The Colosseum

General Knowledge – Round 3 Answers

1. A – In one of the most nauseating TV moments of the year, Holly Willoughby delivered a ninety-second piece to camera about the void left by Phil Schofield, starting with 'Right, deep breath. Firstly, are you OK? I hope so'. Thankfully we were, as nobody really gave a toss.

2. B – A YouTube prankster rigged up a mobile phone to play sex noises while Gary Lineker was presenting live from the *Match of the Day* studio. To stop people getting too aroused, the director kept cutting to a shot of Danny Murphy.

3. C – Chancellor Jeremy Hunt completed the 2023 London Marathon in five hours and twenty-three minutes, which – when adjusted for inflation – was closer to twelve hours.

4. D – Two tree-huggers half-heartedly unfurled a banner urging action on climate change before being gently shuffled offstage by security, and it was by far the most exciting thing that's ever happened during a Keir Starmer speech.

5. D – Nazanin Zaghari-Ratcliffe attended Wimbledon after being invited by Andy Murray, whom she'd watched win the trophy while imprisoned in Iran in 2016. After watching the 2023 version in action though, she conceded that perhaps solitary confinement wasn't so bad after all.

6. B – Hugh Grant was annoyed when interviewer Ashley Graham asked him about *Glass Onion: A Knives Out Mystery* because although he's in it, he's only onscreen for about three seconds. In truth, this interview will probably be forgotten about rather quickly, as if you google 'Hugh Grant awkward

encounter with woman in LA' it brings up a completely different story.

7. B – *Barbie* was banned in Vietnam due to a scene depicting disputed Chinese territorial claims. Long-time fans of Barbie will fondly remember that she divides her time between shopping, going to the beach, and exacerbating geopolitical tensions in South Asia.

8. B – German magazine *Die Aktuelle* published an AI-generated interview with Michael Schumacher, who hasn't been seen in public since being injured in a skiing accident more than nine years ago. The article prompted calls for the media to refrain from any interviews generated by AI, forcing Radio 4 to pull an episode of *Desert Island Discs* with Genghis Khan.

9. A – The screening of a film about Jeremy Corbyn – which trots out the less than peace-loving message that Corbyn was defeated by a conspiracy of Jews – had been due to take place at Glastonbury, because nothing says rock 'n' roll like sitting quietly in a field and watching a documentary about an old man.

10. D – The tourist – a twenty-seven-year-old man from Bristol – who carved his name into Rome's Colosseum claimed that he didn't know it was old, which is fair enough as from certain angles it does look like a new-build.

At Paris Fashion Week, allegations that the catwalk
had been constructed on the cheap were confirmed
to be true at the worst possible moment:

ALL MIXED UP – ROUND 3

One final round of 2023 anagrams to unscramble.

1. LEARNER WOLF (two words) English rugby captain who had a red card controversially rescinded following a match against Wales in August.
2. CARPOOL BABES (two words) Infamous Colombian drug lord. In July it was revealed that he once offered to surrender to authorities if his family could settle in the UK.
3. TOYSO (one word) Silent children's TV character. In July an original hand puppet from the show sold for more than £1,000.
4. KNEEL SHELTON (two words) Former *Blue Peter* and current *Countryfile* presenter. In July she announced live on air that she was stepping down from her show on Radio 5 Live to spend more time with her family.
5. IL WOK (one word) British high-street retailer that called in the administrators in August. You'd go here if you needed boot polish, a lampshade and a metric tonne of pick 'n' mix.
6. HOW TWINES (two words) Titular character from a 1937 Disney film. An upcoming remake caused controversy in 2023 when it was revealed her seven vertically challenged companions had been removed from the title.

7. TABARD TOURS (two words) English cricketer and former One Day and Twenty20 captain. Retired from Test Match cricket in July and bowed out by taking the final wicket of the 2023 Ashes to draw the series with Australia.

8. AFRESH WITHOUT THYME (five words) Netflix reality show which follows the day-to-day life of a charismatic British professional boxer and his family.

9. ALIVE AXE LANNY (two words) Russian opposition leader and anti-corruption (Putin) activist. In July he was sentenced to a further nineteen years in a maximum-security prison.

10. SAWING ARMENIA (two words) Dutch football manager who led England's Lionesses to the World Cup Final in August.

11. ORIENT BORDER (three words) Legendary American actor who turned eighty in August. Films include *Taxi Driver*, *Raging Bull* and *The Deer Hunter*.

12. HARPOONIST JONATHAN-MONKS (three words) British heptathlete who won a gold medal at the World Athletics Championships in Budapest.

13. MOTH YARD (two words) British star of *Peaky Blinders* and *Mad Max: Fury Road*. In July he returned to *CBeebies Bedtime Stories* due to popular demand – mainly from mums rather than children.

14. NOMINATED SHAUN (two words) Film based on a spooky Disney World attraction, starring Owen Wilson, Rosario Dawson and Danny DeVito.

15. GARTH HUNG (two words) Veteran British actor who found himself at the centre of an argument about whether or not he should have been cast as an Oompa-Loompa in 2023's *Wonka*.

16. SOLEMNNESS TORCH (three words) In August and September, enthusiasts carried out the biggest ever search for this mythical aquatic creature.

17. ORANGERY SPRY (two words) English contemporary artist known for his trademark colourful clothes. In June he was knighted by Prince William at Windsor castle while wearing a burgundy taffeta dress.

18. VIGILANT CORN ANTHILL (three words) West London carnival which celebrated its fifty-fifth year in 2023, attracting an estimated two million people to its famous parade.

19. LAYMAN PIE (two words) Former One Direction member (and arguably the least popular) who cancelled his tour of South America in September, citing a kidney infection.

20. AEROSPACE HUBBLE POLLACK (three words) Lancashire-based tourist attraction which was named the eighth best amusement park in the world in the 2023 Tripadvisor Travellers' Choice Awards, beating Universal Studios, Busch Gardens and every single Disney park.

21. WILMA DIV SALAD (two words) British actor, talent show judge and children's author, whose latest novel, *The Blunders*, came out in October.

22. VEAL PLUTO (two words) Gravity-defying athletics event which was jointly won by American Katie Moon and Australian Nina Kennedy after they agreed to share the gold medal at the Budapest World Athletics Championships in August.

23. HAIKU SMUF (one word) Japanese city which suffered a catastrophic nuclear disaster in 2011. It made headlines again in 2023 due to plans to dump millions of tonnes of radioactive water into the ocean.

24. AGREE PENCE (one word) Environmental group/ society of tree huggers whose activists scaled Rishi Sunak's house and covered it in black fabric in August.

25. MINTIER AIM (two words) American football (or soccer, if you're an idiot) team that Lionel Messi joined after leaving Paris Saint-Germain at the end of June.

ALL MIXED UP – ROUND 3 ANSWERS

1. Owen Farrell

2. Pablo Escobar

3. Sooty

4. Helen Skelton

5. Wilko

6. Snow White

7. Stuart Broad

8. *At Home with the Furys*

9. Alexei Navalny

10. Sarina Wiegman

11. Robert De Niro

12. Katarina Johnson-Thompson

13. Tom Hardy

14. *Haunted Mansion*

15. Hugh Grant

16. Loch Ness Monster

17. Grayson Perry

18. Notting Hill Carnival

19. Liam Payne

20. Blackpool Pleasure Beach

21. David Walliams

22. Pole vault

23. Fukushima

24. Greenpeace

25. Inter Miami

NAME THAT LIB DEM LEADER

2023 was a fairly decent year for the Liberal Democrats, with the party picking up 407 seats at the local elections in May, and – thanks to some very boring leaders – managing to avoid any sort of scandal or drama. Since forming in 1988, the party has had eight leaders, but how many can you remember from the dates and clues below? As a bonus, there's even an extra (literal) clue for each one, because let's face it, they're Liberal Democrats, so only incredibly boring people would have a chance of guessing all eight.

1. *(August 2020–present)* Served as Secretary of State for Energy and Climate Change in the coalition government from 2012 to 2015, but now spends most of his time hitting blue props with a hammer.

   Literal clue – Rhymes with 'red gravy'.

2. *(July 2019–December 2019)* The youngest leader of the Liberal Democrats and also the first woman to hold the position, although not for very long as she lost her seat at the 2019 general election and resigned after just five months.

   Literal clue – If you say 'roundabouts' after her surname, it sounds like a phrase used to describe a situation where losses and gains are about even.

3. *(July 2017–July 2019)* Twinkle-toed MP who served as Business Secretary for the entire duration of the coalition government.

   Literal clue – His surname is something which – among other things – carries electricity.

4. *(July 2015–July 2017)* Arguably the least inspiring Lib Dem leader. Tasked with picking up the pieces following the party's disastrous involvement in the coalition government, but often came under scrutiny for his views on LGBT rights.

   Literal clue – Shares a first name with a Harry Enfield character who is nice, but dim.

5. *(December 2007–July 2015)* Former deputy PM under David Cameron, whose political career ended in shame and disgrace, working for Mark Zuckerberg.

   Literal clue – His surname rhymes with something that comes out of the back of a chicken.

6. *(March 2006–October 2007)* Living skeleton who held the British record for the hundred-metre sprint between 1967 and 1974 (although if it took seven years, it can't have been that quick).

   Literal clue – His nickname often precedes 'Dynasty' when talking about priceless vases.

7. *(August 1999–January 2006)* Red-headed leader who oversaw the Liberal Democrats during the 2001 and 2005 general elections. Bon viveur and panel-show regular who clocked up more *Have I Got News for You* appearances than Boris Johnson.

   Literal clue – You might find his surname on a Florida space centre, although it was actually named after somebody else.

8. *(July 1988–August 1999)* The first leader of the party proper following the merger between the Liberal and Social Democratic parties in 1988, and also the longest serving. Actively lobbied for military action against Yugoslavia, and would go on to appear as a witness for the prosecution at the trial of Slobodan Milošević.

   Literal clue – A famous *Sun* headline once gave his surname as 'Pantsdown' amid allegations of an affair with his secretary.

Name That Lib Dem Leader – Answers

1. Ed Davey

2. Jo Swinson

3. Vince Cable

4. Tim Farron

5. Nick Clegg

6. Menzies 'Ming' Campbell

7. Charles Kennedy

8. Paddy Ashdown

WAR AND ORDER

The war (or 'special military operation' if you're A: Russian, or B: a complete imbecile) in Ukraine sadly continued throughout 2023. Can you place these ten historic wars into chronological order?

American Civil War

Hundred Years' War

Vietnam War

Second World War

Crimean War

Korean War

Gulf War

First World War

Iraq War

Russo-Japanese War

War and Order – Answers

1. Hundred Years' War (1337–1453)

2. Crimean War (1853–1856)

3. American Civil War (1861–1865)

4. Russo-Japanese War (1904–1905)

5. First World War (1914–1918)

6. Second World War (1939–1945)

7. Korean War (1950–1953)

8. Vietnam War (1955–1975)

9. Gulf War (1990–1991)

10. Iraq War (2003–2011)

THE EXTREMELY LITERAL INFLATION ROUND

Inflation continued to spiral out of control in 2023, despite the government doing everything it could[*] to keep it down. Inflation in the economic sense is pretty dull, so instead here are sections of six balloons based on fictional characters and/or real people. Can you work out who they're supposed to represent?

1.

2.

---

[*] Absolutely nothing.

3.

4.

5.

6.

The Extremely Literal Inflation Round — Answers

1. Spongebob Squarepants

2. Paddington Bear

3. Donald Trump

4. Spider-Man

5. Tony the Tiger

6. Charlie Brown

GUESS THE GB NEWS PRESENTER

Very few people had faith that GB News would last this long (not least Andrew Neil, who helped to set the channel up in 2021 and almost immediately abandoned ship) but the Poundland of British news channels traversed 2023 with an increasingly ridiculous array of segments, and an even more perplexing roster of hosts. The following clues all relate to people who were named as presenters on GB News in 2023, but how many can you get? This round should be quite easy if you're one of the six people who watch the channel on a regular basis.

1. Nineties pop singer with washboard abs. Formerly married to Katie Price (not that that narrows it down much).

2. Former UK political party leader who spends most of his time flogging gin and standing on beaches and angrily pointing at the sea.

3. Another former political leader, who served as first minister of Northern Ireland from 2016 to 2017, and again from 2020 and 2021. During this time she was also leader of the DUP (2015–2021), and in 2017 she helped prop up Theresa May's government in exchange for a nine-figure boost to NI finances.

4. Former actor and 'musician' who used to be married to Billie Piper, before giving it all up to become an eternally outraged 'social commentator' (whatever that means).

5. Northern Irish broadcaster and former *This Morning* presenter, who gifted GB News with one of its most-watched moments of the year in June after not realising he was on the air and muttering 'Now how the fuck do I get home today?' to fellow presenter Isabel Webster.

6. Conservative MP and former work and pensions secretary who in 2018 faced calls to resign after being accused of misleading MPs over Universal Credit. Presented numerous TV shows in the 1990s, such as *But First This, How Do They Do That?* and *The Heaven and Earth Show*.

7. Former Tory MP who was famously unseated at the 1997 general election. Nowadays spends most of his time riding around on trains and wearing awful trousers.

8. Journalist and broadcaster who worked for the *Sun* and *News of the World*. In 2023 he was accused by the *Byline Times* of using an alias to obtain sexually explicit videos. He appeared on his own programme to deny the allegations.

9. Former *Monty Python* star and vocal supporter of free speech, who divided opinion in 2023 by announcing the return of a beloved 1970s sitcom.

10. Yet another Tory MP, who was knighted in 2023 for services to being blindly loyal to Boris Johnson.

Guess the GB News Presenter – Answers

1. Peter Andre

2. Nigel Farage

3. Arlene Foster

4. Laurence Fox

5. Eamonn Holmes

6. Esther McVey

7. Michael Portillo

8. Dan Wootton

9. John Cleese

10. Jacob Rees-Mogg

MISSING WORDS – ROUND 3

Some more missing words to have a crack at. Can you fill in the blanks?

1. The Dalai Lama apologizes for asking a young boy to

    _____

    NPR – 10 April

    A. Suck his tongue
    B. Massage his feet
    C. Sit on his lap
    D. Call him 'Big Daddy'

2. Couple take revenge on Airbnb host by _____ for 25 days

    Independent – 19 April

    A. Having noisy sex
    B. Not flushing the toilet
    C. Leaving taps running and gas on
    D. Cooking nothing but fish

3. Man set to complete visiting all 875 _____
   in Britain and Ireland this week
   The Yorkshireman – 6 June

   A. Post offices

   B. Wetherspoon pubs

   C. Amusement arcades

   D. Post offices

4. New Forest introduces £1,000 fine for tourists who
   _____

   Express – 14 April

   A. Climb trees

   B. Swim in the nude

   C. Urinate outside

   D. Bother wild ponies

5. Ed Sheeran warns he'll _____ if found
   guilty in copyright trial
   NME – 2 May

   A. Quit music

   B. Shave his head

   C. Buy the rights to Marvin Gaye's back catalogue

   D. Perform a dirty protest

6. Priti Patel unveils memorial bench for _____ 'brutally' killed in Essex pond
Essex Live – 26 April

   A. Swans

   B. Cat

   C. Koi carp

   D. Heron

7. Hundreds of pounds of _____ mysteriously dumped in New Jersey woods
CBS News – 4 May

   A. Melted cheese

   B. Dead crickets

   C. Anchovies

   D. Cooked pasta

8. Woolshed nightclub apologises for urging patrons to _____ for free drinks
ABC News – 5 June

   A. Punch each other in the face

   B. Snort salt

   C. Take off bras

   D. Send abusive texts

9. _____

top celeb sex doll requests
New York Post – 19 April

   A. Nigella Lawson, Holly Willoughby and Claudia Winkleman

   B. George Clooney, Jake Gyllenhaal and Tom Hardy

   C. Princess Diana, Kate Middleton and Meghan Markle

   D. Keir Starmer, Tony Blair and Jeremy Corbyn

10. Three rescued after _____ drifts out to sea off Devon coast
Guardian – 8 June

   A. Inflatable duck

   B. Banana boat

   C. Picnic table

   D. Rubber shark

MISSING WORDS – ROUND 3 ANSWERS

1. A – The Dalai Lama apologizes for asking a young boy to **suck his tongue**. In April a clip was posted online that showed the Dalai Lama asking a child to suck his tongue, drawing widespread criticism from almost everyone, with the exception of the Catholic Church, which remained completely silent on the matter for some reason.

2. C – Couple take revenge on Airbnb host by **leaving taps running and gas on** for 25 days. A Korean couple who were unable to cancel their booking travelled to the property in Seoul anyway to leave the gas and taps running for the twenty-five days that they'd originally planned to stay. The owner was left with an energy bill equivalent to £1,000, which in the UK works out to roughly the same as boiling three eggs.

3. B – Man set to complete visiting all 875 **Wetherspoon pubs** in Britain and Ireland this week. The sixty-year-old from Derby completed the feat by visiting the Wetherspoon pub in the South Terminal at Gatwick airport which requires customers to show their flight booking, or pilot's licence.

4. D – New Forest introduces £1,000 fine for tourists who **bother wild ponies**. The fine was introduced to stop people petting ponies in order to protect them from 'serious harm', and to avoid a repeat of what happened to Shetland ponies, which used to be a lot taller before people started patting them.

5. A – Ed Sheeran warns he'll **quit music** if found guilty in copyright trial. He did of course end up winning the court case brought by the family of Marvin Gaye, but not before offering the world this brief glimpse of hope.

6. A – Priti Patel unveils memorial bench for **swans** 'brutally' killed in Essex pond. Priti Patel unveiled a bench in Coggeshall, Essex which was installed as a tribute to four swans reportedly killed by catapults and, as a mark of respect, the former home secretary lowered her smirk to half-mast.

7. D – Hundreds of pounds of **cooked pasta** mysteriously dumped in New Jersey woods. Police were baffled following the discovery of more than five hundred pounds of cooked pasta next to a river in the town of Old Bridge, New Jersey in May, but said it was more than likely a prank carried out by a fusilli individuals.

8. C – Woolshed nightclub apologises for urging patrons to **take off bras** for free drinks. To make matters worse, the nightclub in Adelaide, Australia offered more free drinks for people who handed in larger cup sizes than those who handed in A and B cups. Fingers crossed this promotion finds its way to the UK, as a bra is considerably cheaper than a pint when you get south of Milton Keynes.

9. C – **Princess Diana, Kate Middleton and Meghan Markle** top celeb sex doll requests. If you own one of these, good luck explaining it to the wife you definitely haven't got.

10. A – Three rescued after **inflatable duck** drifts out to sea off Devon coast. The RNLI rescued three people when a huge inflatable duck that they were sitting on was carried out to sea in early June. Luckily it had been a strong month for donations, which allowed rescuers to pick up the enormous bill.

At King Charles's coronation, a barefoot Prince Louis found out the hard way why his parents are always telling him to stop leaving Lego on the royal balcony:

Higher Education

In May, Jeremy Paxman stepped down from hosting *University Challenge* after almost twenty-nine years, handing over the reins to Amol Rajan. Can you place the following university towns and cities on a map of Britain?

1. Oxford
2. Cambridge
3. Cardiff
4. Exeter
5. Edinburgh
6. Manchester
7. Durham
8. Belfast
9. Leeds
10. St Andrews

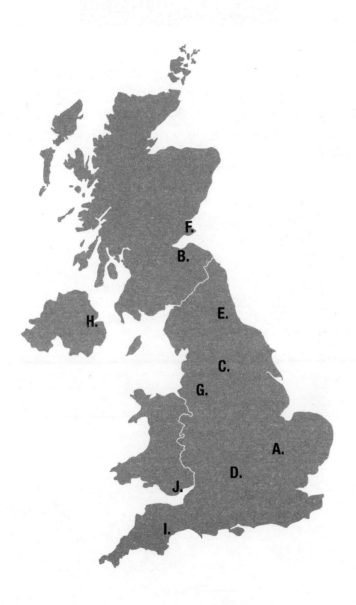

Higher Education – Answers

F. St Andrews

B. Edinburgh

H. Belfast

E. Durham

C. Leeds

G. Manchester

A. Cambridge

D. Oxford

J. Cardiff

I. Exeter

SONG 3

Britpop made an unlikely comeback in 2023 as Blur scored a number-one album and played two sold-out shows at Wembley Stadium. The answers to this round are all British bands who are also synonymous with the nineties, but can you name them from the titles of three of their songs?

1. Common People, Do You Remember the First Time?, Disco 2000

    A.   The Charlatans
    B.   Pulp
    C.   Ash
    D.   The Bluetones

2. Why Does It Always Rain on Me?, Driftwood, Sing

    A.   Travis
    B.   Kula Shaker
    C.   Dodgy
    D.   Cornershop

3. The Bartender and the Thief, Dakota, Have a Nice Day

    A. Mansun

    B. Shed Seven

    C. Embrace

    D. Stereophonics

4. Live Forever, Stand by Me, She's Electric

    A. Super Furry Animals

    B. Oasis

    C. The Boo Radleys

    D. Elastica

5. Creep, No Surprises, Paranoid Android

    A. Catatonia

    B. Supergrass

    C. The Divine Comedy

    D. Radiohead

6. Lucky Man, The Drugs Don't Work, Bitter Sweet Symphony

    A. The Verve

    B. Keane

    C. The Lightning Seeds

    D. Black Grape

7. A Design for Life, Motorcycle Emptiness, If You Tolerate This Your Children Will Be Next

    A. Skunk Anansie

    B. Manic Street Preachers

    C. Sleeper

    D. The Wildhearts

8. Trash, Beautiful Ones, Animal Nitrate

    A. Suede

    B. Babylon Zoo

    C. Inspiral Carpets

    D. Reef

9. The Day We Caught the Train, The Riverboat Song, Hundred Mile High City

    A. Placebo

    B. Chumbawamba

    C. Texas

    D. Ocean Colour Scene

10. Female of the Species, Neighbourhood, The Ballad of Tom Jones

    A. Garbage

    B. The Levellers

    C. Space

    D. Republica

Song 3 – Answers

1. B – Pulp

2. A – Travis

3. D – Stereophonics

4. B – Oasis

5. D – Radiohead

6. A – The Verve

7. B – Manic Street Preachers

8. A – Suede

9. D – Ocean Colour Scene

10. C – Space

REAL OR FAKE HARRY POTTER CHARACTER?

J.K. Rowling divided opinion once more in 2023 due to her views on trans rights, and a chart-topping podcast called *The Witch Trials of J.K. Rowling*, but a round on that would never get signed off by legal. Luckily she used to be known for writing books about a jaunty little wizard, so here's one about that instead. Below are twenty names, but are they actual characters from the Harry Potter universe, or just made-up nonsense?

1. Cedric Diggory
2. Ludo Bagman
3. Bathilda Bagshot
4. Hector Grimsniff
5. Fenrir Greyback
6. Prendergast Toggle
7. Bellatrix Lestrange
8. Arteus Dump
9. Luna Lovegood
10. Rita Skeeter
11. Crowphelia Vargus
12. Nymphadora Tonks
13. Norton Antivirus
14. Serendipity Tombola
15. Cuthbert Binns
16. Grompton Numpty
17. Petunia Merryweather
18. Robert Pegglesworth
19. Silvanus Kettleburn
20. Jeremy Artichoke

REAL OR FAKE HARRY POTTER CHARACTER? – ANSWERS

Real

1. Cedric Diggory

2. Ludo Bagman

3. Bathilda Bagshot

5. Fenrir Greyback

7. Bellatrix Lestrange

9. Luna Lovegood

10. Rita Skeeter

12. Nymphadora Tonks

15. Cuthbert Binns

19. Silvanus Kettleburn

Not real

4. Hector Grimsniff

6. Prendergast Toggle

8. Arteus Dump

11. Crowphelia Vargus

13. Norton Antivirus

14. Serendipity Tombola

16. Grompton Numpty

17. Petunia Merryweather

18. Robert Pegglesworth

20. Jeremy Artichoke

SPEED ROUND 2

Another speedy round with two possible answers per question. Wrong answers add five seconds.

Less than ninety seconds – top of the class

Ninety seconds to two and a half minutes – two house points

Two and a half minutes to four minutes – must try harder

Longer than four minutes – detention

1. In May, actor Derek Thompson announced that he'd be stepping down from which TV show after playing the character of Charlie Fairhead for thirty-seven years?

   Emmerdale / Casualty

2. In July, Rihanna became the first female artist to have ten different songs with a billion or more streams on Spotify. Which household object was the title of her first UK number one in 2007?

   Umbrella / Lightbulb

3. During the second Test of the 2023 Ashes, which England cricketer was controversially stumped after wandering away from his crease?

   Jonny Bairstow / Ben Stokes

4. Rail strikes continued throughout 2023, headed up by the smooth-headed general secretary of the RMT. What is his name?

Mick Lynch / Dick Pinch

5. 2023 was Mark Rowley's first full year as commissioner of the Met Police. What was the name of his predecessor?

Cassandra Deck / Cressida Dick

6. In March, which disgraced former pop star was recalled to prison after just six weeks for breaching his licence conditions?

Rolf Harris / Gary Glitter

7. In June, Southern, Thameslink and Gatwick Express rail services introduced a ban on what, due to concerns over fire risk?

Vaping / E-scooters

8. Which driver won the 2023 Formula 1 British Grand Prix?

Lewis Hamilton / Max Verstappen

9. According to the *Mirror*, Ed Sheeran, Adele, Kylie Minogue and Elton John all turned down invitations to perform at which music event?

   The Coronation Concert / The Royal Variety Performance

10. In June, Prince William launched a scheme aiming to reduce homelessness in the UK with which former Spice Girl?

    Geri Horner / Victoria Beckham

11. In July, which girl group became the first ever Korean act to headline a UK festival at London's BST Hyde Park?

    BLACKPINK / Red Velvet

12. Guillermo del Toro's reimagining of which nineteenth-century children's story won Best Animated Film at the 2023 Golden Globes?

    Treasure Island / Pinocchio

13. Which legendary American football player – with seven Super Bowl titles to his name – announced his retirement in February at the age of forty-five?

    Dan Marino / Tom Brady

14. In April, Royal Mail increased the price of what by fifteen pence?

    A4 Jiffy bags / First-class stamps

15. In July, Ant and Dec confirmed that which British teen drama – which aired between 1989 and 2006 – was to be revived?

    Grange Hill / *Byker Grove*

16. Which two southern hemisphere countries co-hosted the 2023 FIFA Women's World Cup?

    Australia and New Zealand / Argentina and Chile

17. In March, the Parliamentary Standards Committee recommended that SNP MP Margaret Ferrier should be suspended from the Commons for thirty days for doing what in September 2020?

    Breaching Covid rules / Misreporting her expenses

18. In July, Mark Zuckerberg's Meta launched a text-based, Twitter-style app to compete with Elon Musk's failing platform. What is it called?

    Telegram / Threads

19. One of 2023's most critically panned TV shows was *The Idol*, which stars Lily-Rose Depp and which Canadian singer?

The Weeknd / Bryan Adams

20. British band The 1975 were banned from playing in which country after a festival appearance in July which saw frontman Matty Healy kiss bass player Ross MacDonald in an apparent act of defiance at strict anti-LGBTQ+ laws?

Malaysia / Pakistan

SPEED ROUND 2 – ANSWERS

1. *Casualty*

2. Umbrella

3. Jonny Bairstow

4. Mick Lynch

5. Cressida Dick

6. Gary Glitter

7. E-scooters

8. Max Verstappen

9. The Coronation Concert

10. Geri Horner

11. BLACKPINK

12. *Pinocchio*

13. Tom Brady

14. First-class stamps

15. *Byker Grove*

16. Australia and New Zealand

17. Breaching Covid rules

18. Threads

19. The Weeknd

20. Malaysia

SLOW NEWS ~~DAY~~ YEAR

With Rishi Sunak, Keir Starmer and Ed Davey heading up the UK's main political parties, it was never going to be a particularly exhilarating year, but some of 2023's headlines from mainstream news outlets were among the dullest ever seen. Can you work out which of the following boring headlines were published in 2023, and which are completely made up?

1. Norfolk beach walker finds crisp packet from 1960s

2. Uber Eats customer bemused after ordering 100 free sauce packets – only to be charged £15

3. Couple who paid £950 for 'pregnant' dog discover that it is just very fat

4. Woman who despises Pot Noodles to eat ten of them for charity

5. Couples weekend away 'ruined' as man turned away at restaurant due to 'open toe' sandals

6. Yorkshire restaurant receives first one-star Tripadvisor review in fifteen years

7. 14-dog conga line breaks Guinness World Record in Germany

8. Married couple choose not to have same surname – because their first and middle names are identical

9. Peter Andre lookalike leaves hen party after just four minutes due to 'lewd comments' from bride's mother

10. Man buys fifteen cordless drills for just £10 due to IT glitch

11. Low Traffic Neighbourhoods: Is this the UK's most abused traffic bollard?

12. Cyclist who broke nose on hanging basket to take legal action after losing sense of smell

13. Tenant who installed artificial grass inside flat ordered to pay for new carpet

14. I'm pregnant with triplets and my bump is so huge I can barely drive my car

15. Gary Barlow admits astonishing fact that he's not eaten a hamburger in 14 years

16. School defends 'vegan' lunch that contained six eggs

17. Nintendo Switch missing during hotel stay in Norwich

18. Strange but true: tarot cards accurately predict dad-of-three being hit by a tractor

19. Is this the world's greatest gate? The Gate Appreciation Society thinks so

20. Residents' outrage as bin men arrive at 4 a.m. for second week running

21. Asda apologises after mum 'disgusted' with fish fingers

22. Dad fumes after he was 'ignored' and had to wait eight minutes for McDonald's grub

23. Man who paid for extra legroom on Ryanair flight given regular seat

24. King Charles left red-faced as he reveals giant hole in his sock at royal engagement

25. Monty Don apologises after being pictured buying peated compost at Hertfordshire garden centre

26. Liam Gallagher buys battered sausage in chippy

27. Saving expert says people can save up to £15 a year by buying pyjama tops and bottoms separately

28. Police investigating anti-social behaviour after group seen doing motorbike wheelies along Hull road

29. McDonald's drive-thru worker loses job after throwing more than ten thousand paper straws in the bin

30. Dunelm apologises to customers after popular cushion sells out within minutes

SLOW NEWS ~~DAY~~ YEAR – ANSWERS

Real Boring Headlines

1. Norfolk beach walker finds crisp packet from 1960s (BBC – 16 May)

2. Uber Eats customer bemused after ordering 100 free sauce packets – only to be charged £15 (*Mirror* – 9 May)

5. Couples weekend away 'ruined' as man turned away at restaurant due to 'open toe' sandals (*Daily Express* – 13 May)

7. 14-dog conga line breaks Guinness World Record in Germany (*New York Post* – 4 February)

8. Married couple choose not to have same surname – because their first and middle names are identical (*Manchester Evening News* – 1 May)

11. Low Traffic Neighbourhoods: Is this the UK's most abused traffic bollard? (BBC – 17 April)

14. I'm pregnant with triplets and my bump is so huge that I can barely drive my car (Mail Online – 18 July)

15. Gary Barlow admits astonishing fact that he's not eaten a hamburger in 14 years (*Metro* – 15 July)

17. Nintendo Switch missing during hotel stay in Norwich (*Eastern Daily Press* – 15 February)

19. Is this the world's greatest gate? The Gate Appreciation Society thinks so (*Guardian* – 17 April)

21. Asda apologises after mum 'disgusted' with fish fingers (*Liverpool Echo* – 3 April)

22. Dad fumes after he was 'ignored' and had to wait eight minutes for McDonald's grub (*Daily Star* – 20 Feb)

24. King Charles left red-faced as he reveals giant hole in his sock at royal engagement (*OK!* magazine – 9 February)

26. Liam Gallagher buys battered sausage in chippy (BBC – 12 May)

28. Police investigating anti-social behaviour after group seen doing motorbike wheelies along Hull road (ITV News – 19 February)

Fake Boring Headlines

3. Couple who paid £950 for 'pregnant' dog discover that it is just very fat

4. Woman who despises Pot Noodles to eat ten of them for charity

6. Yorkshire restaurant receives first one-star Tripadvisor review in fifteen years.

9. Peter Andre lookalike leaves hen party after just four minutes due to 'lewd comments' from bride's mother

10. Man buys fifteen cordless drills for just £10 due to IT glitch

12. Cyclist who broke nose on hanging basket to take legal action after losing sense of smell

13. Tenant who installed artificial grass inside flat ordered to pay for new carpet

16. School defends 'vegan' lunch that contained six eggs

18. Strange but true: tarot cards accurately predict dad-of-three being hit by a tractor

20. Residents' outrage as bin men arrive at 4 a.m. for second week running

23. Man who paid for extra legroom on Ryanair flight given regular seat

25. Monty Don apologises after being pictured buying peated compost at Hertfordshire garden centre

27. Saving expert says people can save up to £15 a year by buying pyjama tops and bottoms separately

29. McDonald's drive-thru worker loses job after throwing more than ten thousand paper straws in the bin

30. Dunelm apologises to customers after popular cushion sells out within minutes

TRUE OR FALSE – ROUND 3

You've got a 50 per cent chance of getting these right, so even if you just guess you should score around half.

1. In February, police in Peru found an eight-hundred-year-old mummified corpse inside a food delivery bag.
2. In April, an episode of *Escape to the Country* received seventy-five complaints after social media users noticed that one of the house hunters had not one, but three Nazi tattoos.
3. On New Year's Day a Just Stop Oil activist had to be rescued from a disabled toilet at the World Darts Championship after being chased down by a mob of drunken fans.
4. The UK's first 'driverless' buses launched in May, but require two members of staff on board at all times.
5. During HS2 excavations at London Euston in January, archaeologists discovered a partially intact stegosaurus skeleton.
6. During the writers' strike that took place in the US this year, an entire series of *Law and Order* was written by AI, but after a furious backlash the scripts were destroyed.
7. In May, a student flew from Bristol to Manchester via Zimbabwe as it was £30 cheaper than going by train.
8. New York's Flatiron Building was sold for $191 million at auction in March, but the sale fell through when the winning bidder failed to make the down payment.

9. When final proposals for electoral map boundary changes were released in June, a clerical error led to sixty square feet of Anglesey being listed as a single constituency, despite nobody even living there.

10. A proposed reboot of *Rupert Bear* was shelved early in the year after both scriptwriters made controversial comments about the Holocaust.

11. In March, Ukraine released an air raid app that featured Mark Hamill warning of incoming Russian bombardments in the style of Luke Skywalker.

12. In June, a pencil thought to have belonged to Adolf Hitler sold for more than £5,000 at an auction in Belfast.

13. In August, Oliver Cromwell's great-great-great-great-great-great-great-great-great-great-great-great grandson was arrested for stealing jeans from River Island.

14. In March, Richard Madeley was criticised after seemingly comparing climate activists to paedophiles.

15. During the filming of Prime Video's *The Grand Tour* in March, Richard Hammond ran over James May's foot with a Reliant Robin, breaking four bones.

16. During an interview on a Times Radio podcast in June, Michael Gove admitted that he smoked marijuana at Oxford University, but didn't get very high as drugs were weaker in the 1980s.

17. In March, mathematicians unveiled a thirteen-sided shape which can fill an infinite surface without a single repeating pattern.

18. During US singer Pink's concert at BST Hyde Park in June, a fan threw their dead mother's ashes onto the stage.

19. For Valentine's Day, Yankee Candle released a special edition candle that had lingerie tucked inside the top of the jar, but had to recall them after multiple reports of accidental arsonists not noticing the lingerie and lighting the candle.

20. In January, a seventy-six-year-old conker enthusiast from Staffordshire announced that he was donating part of his ten thousand-strong collection to Ukraine.

TRUE OR FALSE – ROUND 3 ANSWERS

True

1. In February, police in Peru found an eight-hundred-year-old mummified corpse inside a food delivery bag.

4. The UK's first 'driverless' buses launched in May, but require two members of staff on board at all times.

8. New York's Flatiron Building was sold for $191 million at auction in March, but the sale fell through when the winning bidder failed to make the down payment.

11. In March, Ukraine released an air raid app that featured Mark Hamill warning of incoming Russian bombardments in the style of Luke Skywalker.

12. In June, a pencil thought to have belonged to Adolf Hitler sold for more than £5,000 at an auction in Belfast.

14. In March, Richard Madeley was criticised after seemingly comparing climate activists to paedophiles.

16. During an interview on a Times Radio podcast in June, Michael Gove admitted that he smoked marijuana at Oxford University, but didn't get very high as drugs were weaker in the 1980s.

17. In March, mathematicians unveiled a thirteen-sided shape which can fill an infinite surface without a single repeating pattern.

18. During US singer Pink's concert at BST Hyde Park in June, a fan threw their dead mother's ashes onto the stage.

20. In January a seventy-six-year-old conker enthusiast from Staffordshire announced that he was donating part of his ten thousand-strong collection to Ukraine.

False

2. An episode of *Escape to the Country* didn't feature a house hunter with Nazi tattoos.

3. A Just Stop Oil activist wasn't rescued from a disabled toilet at the World Darts Championship

5. Archaeologists didn't discover a stegosaurus skeleton at London Euston.

6. AI didn't produce an entire series of *Law and Order*.

7. A student didn't fly from Bristol to Manchester via Zimbabwe as it was cheaper than going by train.

9. A tiny, uninhabited section of Anglesey wasn't listed as a constituency following boundary changes.

10. A proposed reboot of *Rupert Bear* wasn't shelved due to holocaust comments.

13. Oliver Cromwell's great-great-great-great-great-great-great-great-great-great-great-great grandson wasn't arrested for stealing jeans from River Island.

15. Richard Hammond didn't run over James May's foot with a Reliant Robin.

19. Yankee Candle didn't release a special edition candle with lingerie tucked inside.

ODD ONE OUT – ROUND 2

Four more things, but which one doesn't belong, and why?

1.

A: The M25

B: The World Snooker Championship

C: The RHS Chelsea Flower Show

D: The London Marathon

2.

A: Vladimir Putin

B: Nicola Sturgeon

C: Donald Trump

D: Greta Thunberg

ODD ONE OUT – ROUND 2 ANSWERS

1. D – The London Marathon is the odd one out. The other three were all targeted by climate protestors in 2023, whereas organisers of the London Marathon held talks with protest groups beforehand to seek assurances that they wouldn't disrupt the event. It's only right that the others were targeted though, as it's about time someone stood up to the massive carbon footprints of snooker and gardening.

2. A – Vladimir Putin is the odd one out. The other three were all detained by police at some point in 2023 (Sturgeon in June, Trump in April and June, and Thunberg in January and July) whereas Putin – despite the International Criminal Court issuing an arrest warrant for him in March – has continued to steer clear of consequences of any kind. From a logistical point of view, Donald Trump's arrest was the trickiest, with authorities deciding against handcuffs after police pointed out that even on the tightest setting they'd just slide off.

Labour Frontbencher or 1986 Commonwealth Games Medallist?

You'd be forgiven for looking at the title to this one and thinking, 'That's ridiculous, how is anyone supposed to remember the name of a Labour frontbencher?' but they can't all be easy (plus they'll soon be your masters). The people below either served in Keir Starmer's shadow cabinet in 2023 or made the podium at the 1986 Commonwealth Games in Edinburgh. Can you separate them?

1. Bridget Phillipson
2. Ben Johnson
3. Wes Streeting
4. Steven Redgrave
5. Tessa Sanderson
6. Pat McFadden
7. Thangam Debbonaire
8. Lisa Nandy
9. Lennox Lewis
10. Kirsty Wade
11. Alan Campbell
12. Tom McKean
13. Jenny Chapman
14. Preet Kaur Gill
15. Greg Fasala
16. Ian Dickison
17. Paul Curran
18. Louise Haigh
19. Sarah Hardcastle
20. Nick Thomas-Symonds

LABOUR FRONTBENCHER OR 1986 COMMONWEALTH GAMES MEDALLIST? – ANSWERS

Frontbenchers

1. **Bridget Phillipson** *(Shadow Secretary of State for Education)*

3. **Wes Streeting** *(Shadow Secretary of State for Health and Social Care)*

6. **Pat McFadden** *(Shadow Chief Secretary to HM Treasury)*

7. **Thangam Debbonaire** *(Shadow Leader of the House of Commons)*

8. **Lisa Nandy** *(Shadow Secretary of State for Levelling Up, Housing, Communities & Local Government)*

11. **Alan Campbell** *(Opposition Chief Whip in the House of Commons)*

13. **Jenny Chapman** *(Shadow Minister of State at the Cabinet Office)*

14. **Preet Kaur Gill** *(Shadow Cabinet Minister for International Development)*

18. **Louise Haigh** *(Shadow Secretary of State for Transport)*

20. **Nick Thomas-Symonds** *(Shadow Secretary of State for International Trade)*

1986 Commonwealth Games Medallists

2. **Ben Johnson** (Canada) Athletics – two gold, one bronze

4. **Steven Redgrave** (England) Rowing – three gold

5. **Tessa Sanderson** (England) Athletics – gold

9. **Lennox Lewis** (Canada) Boxing – gold

10. **Kirsty Wade** (Wales) Athletics – two gold

12. **Tom McKean** (Scotland) Athletics – silver

15. **Greg Fasala** (Australia) Swimming – two gold, one bronze

16. **Ian Dickison** (New Zealand) Lawn bowls – gold

17. **Paul Curran** (England) Cycling – two gold

19. **Sarah Hardcastle** (England) Swimming – two gold, one silver, one bronze

2023 IN NUMBERS

The answers to the following maths problems all relate to something from 2023. No calculators, or – in the extremely unlikely event that Jacob Rees-Mogg is reading this – abacuses allowed.

1. $250 \times 4 + 100 - 37 =$ Seats lost by the Conservatives at the local elections in May.

2. $1140 \div 3 =$ Words spoken by Keanu Reeves in *John Wick: Chapter 4*, which has a running time of almost three hours.

3. $12 \times 12 - 3 =$ Age (in years) that scientists claimed humans could one day reach, according to the results of an American study in March.

4. $5{,}000 \div 25 =$ Distance (in kilometres) that the Wagner mercenary group was from Moscow when they agreed to turn back on 24 June, after leader Yevgeny Prigozhin struck a deal with Belarusian president Alexander Lukashenko to call off the advance.

5. $5 \times 8 - (36 \div 6) =$ Number of felonies that Donald Trump was charged with in March, following his arrest.

6. $9 \times 11 - (4 \times 5) =$ Actor Robert De Niro's age when he became a father for the seventh time, in May.

7. $\sqrt{16} + 1 =$ The number of key pledges that Rishi Sunak announced in January, which he almost definitely won't achieve.

8. $10.1 \times 1{,}000$ = Cost (in British pounds) of the most expensive compartment aboard the *Orient Express*, which axed its UK section in 2023 after forty-one years.

9. $90 \div 6 - 15$ = Number of British singles players who advanced to the second week of Wimbledon.

10. $500 - 125 - 250 - 124$ = The amount (in British pounds) that online estate agent Strike paid to purchase rival Purple Bricks in May.

11. $175 \times 20 - 1$ = Price (in US dollars) of Apple's widely mocked Vision Pro headset, which was unveiled in June.

12. $200 \times 7 + (3 \times 20) + 1$ = Height (in feet) of a proposed flagpole in Maine, USA which was announced in July and which – if built – will be the tallest in the world.

13. $\sqrt{121}$ = Nominations achieved by *Everything Everywhere All at Once* at the 2023 Academy Awards.

14. $4 \times 4 \times 4 + 18$ = Age of Miriam Margolyes when she made her *Vogue* cover debut in July.

15. 48×50 = Amount (in British pounds) that Labour said it would give to new teachers to try to stop them leaving the profession, if they win the next election.

2023 in Numbers – Answers

1. Seats lost by the Conservatives at the local elections in May = 1,063

2. Words spoken by Keanu Reeves in *John Wick: Chapter 4*, which has a running time of almost three hours = 380

3. Age (in years) that scientists claimed humans could one day reach, according to the results of an American study in March = 141

4. Distance (in kilometres) that the Wagner mercenary group was from Moscow when they agreed to turn back on 24 June, after leader Yevgeny Prigozhin struck a deal with Belarusian president Alexander Lukashenko to call off the advance = 200

5. Number of felonies that Donald Trump was charged with following his arrest in March = 34

6. Actor Robert De Niro's age when he became a father for the seventh time in May = 79

7. The number of key pledges that Rishi Sunak announced in January, which he almost definitely won't achieve = 5

8. Cost (in British pounds) of the most expensive compartment aboard the *Orient Express*, which axed its UK section in 2023 after forty-one years = 10,100

9. Number of British singles players who advanced to the second week of Wimbledon 2023 = 0

10. Amount (in British pounds) that online estate agent Strike paid to purchase rival Purple Bricks in May = 1

11. Price (in US dollars) of Apple's widely mocked Vision Pro headset, which was unveiled in June = 3,499

12. Height (in feet) of a proposed flagpole in Maine, USA which was announced in July and which – if built – will be the tallest in the world = 1,461

13. Nominations achieved by *Everything Everywhere All at Once* at the 2023 Oscars = 11

14. Age of Miriam Margolyes when she made her *Vogue* cover debut in July = 82

15. Amount (in British pounds) that Labour said it would give to new teachers to try and stop them leaving the profession, if they win the next election = 2,400

LIGHT-HEARTED DESPOT WORDSEARCH

In June, Belarusian nutcase Alexander Lukashenko came to fellow despot Vladimir Putin's aid by convincing mercenary boss Yevgeny Prigozhin to call off his march on Moscow. Below are the surnames of several other unhinged, power-mad leaders, but can you find them in this delightfully light-hearted wordsearch?

1. Mussolini
2. Stalin
3. Pinochet
4. Amin
5. Hussein
6. Gaddafi
7. Pot
8. Franco
9. Batista
10. Hitler

```
P  Q  T  T  K  I  N  Q  F  K  E  K  S  X  Y  R  I  Y
G  A  E  X  X  E  F  M  R  S  C  N  T  X  W  S  Q  H
J  M  W  G  E  S  M  R  I  P  Q  B  R  X  N  R  U  P
F  I  X  Z  M  K  F  U  A  A  I  L  A  A  H  K  S  I
P  N  J  V  O  V  N  I  S  N  C  N  J  T  C  O  R  V
H  Q  P  W  X  N  F  R  I  S  C  X  O  Z  I  P  A  U
I  W  E  I  T  S  X  T  L  E  O  O  C  C  D  S  J  F
T  Y  Q  C  D  S  T  A  L  I  N  L  B  F  H  I  T  I
L  G  S  F  F  N  V  N  Y  O  H  V  I  P  Q  E  W  A
E  J  R  Z  J  H  U  S  S  E  I  N  O  N  O  G  T  P
R  R  K  N  B  W  A  N  Y  X  P  B  P  M  I  T  N  C
F  R  Z  G  A  D  D  A  F  I  W  N  Z  R  N  T  A  D
```

Light-hearted Despot
Wordsearch – Solution

```
.   .   .   .   .   .   .   .   .   .   .   .   .   .   .
.   A   .   .   .   F   .   .   .   .   .   .   .   .   .
.   M   .   .   .   M   R   .   P   .   B   .   .   .   .
.   I   .   .   .   .   U   A   .   I   .   A   .   .   .
.   N   .   .   .   .   .   S   N   .   N   .   T   .   .
H   .   .   .   .   .   .   S   C   .   O   .   I   .   .
I   .   .   .   .   .   .   .   O   O   .   C   .   S   .
T   .   .   .   S   T   A   L   I   N   L   .   .   H   .   T
L   .   .   .   .   .   .   .   .   .   .   I   P   .   E   .   A
E   .   .   .   .   H   U   S   S   E   I   N   .   N   O   .   T
R   .   .   .   .   .   .   .   .   .   .   .   I   T   .   .
.   .   .   G   A   D   D   A   F   I   .   .   .   .   .   .
```

General Knowledge – Round 4

Ten more general knowledge questions to get your teeth into.

1. In May, Shadow Chancellor Rachel Reeves flew to the US to discuss Labour's economic plans, but the trip was overshadowed by a tweet she deleted, which included a photo of her doing what?

    A. Posing with a Confederate statue
    B. Defacing a government poster
    C. Travelling in business class
    D. Drinking wine straight from the bottle

2. During a live event on 5 June, Apple revealed that it was making which long-requested update to its products?

    A. A quieter version of loudspeaker for use on public transport
    B. The ability to charge using solar power
    C. An option for autocorrect to ignore the word 'fuck'
    D. The return of traditional headphone jacks

3. On 19 April police warned that what would cause a wave of crime in central London?

    A. The legalisation of cocaine
    B. Late-night pub openings for King Charles's coronation
    C. A twenty-four-hour Greggs
    D. Replacing PCSOs with robots

4. A Scottish runner who placed third at the GB Ultras Manchester–Liverpool fifty-mile race on 7 April was disqualified when it emerged that she'd done what during the race?

    A. Taken a shortcut
    B. Assaulted a fellow runner
    C. Robbed a petrol station
    D. Used a car

5. In June, what was blamed for an unexpected inflation spike in Sweden?

    A. The war in Ukraine
    B. A shortage of beans
    C. A new version of *Minecraft*
    D. A Beyoncé concert

6. In July, China's Hangzhou Zoo enjoyed a 30 per cent rise in visitors after what claim was made about some of its bears?

    A. They were actually humans in disguise
    B. Touching them brought seven years' good luck
    C. They could perform traditional dance styles
    D. They had taught themselves how to speak to humans

7. One of the government's grand plans to clamp down on illegal immigration in 2023 involved housing asylum seekers on a rusty barge off the coast of Dorset. What is it called?

    A. *Bobby Copenhagen*
    B. *Libby Bratislava*
    C. *Bibby Stockholm*
    D. *Nobby Bucharest*

8. In late August, six children and two adults were dramatically rescued in Pakistan after becoming trapped in what?

    A. Rollercoaster
    B. Cable car
    C. Monorail
    D. Waltzer

9. In September, a version of which toy was released with blind and partially sighted children in mind?

    A. Barbie
    B. Scalextric
    C. Lego
    D. Furby

10. In August, two people were left with minor injuries at the Carfest motor show in Hampshire after an accident involving which celebrity and vehicle combo?

    A. Chris Evans in a tuk-tuk
    B. Jonathan Ross in a hovercraft
    C. Jessie Wallace on an e-scooter
    D. Chris Eubank in a go-kart

General Knowledge – Round 4 Answers

1. C – Rachel Reeves deleted a tweet which showed her travelling in a business class seat with a reported cost of £4,000, leading to claims of hypocrisy from the *Express* and *Daily Mail*. It's terrifying to think that you could fork out four grand for a flight and end up sitting next to a Labour MP.

2. C – During Apple's 2023 Worldwide Developers Conference, the company revealed that its new autocorrect software would no longer change 'fuck' and 'fucking' to 'duck' and 'ducking'. Still no word on a charger cable that lasts longer than thirty minutes before snapping, but at least when it falls apart you can send an expletive-filled text to customer service.

3. C – Police warned that a proposed twenty-four-hour Greggs in Leicester Square would cause a wave of crime, although any criminal who buys sausage rolls at three in the morning is highly unlikely to be able to escape on foot.

4. D – The forty-seven-year-old runner from Dumfries accepted the trophy for third place but was then disqualified when it transpired that she'd used a car. The whole affair raises a lot of questions, not least who are those two women who can run faster than a car?

5. D – Swedish economists said a Beyoncé concert in Stockholm was partly to blame for an unexpected spike in inflation (she played eight dates in the UK, in case you're wondering why a pint of milk costs fifty quid).

6. A – Viral videos appeared to depict Hangzhou's sun bears as humans in disguise, an allegation that the zoo – and several bears – vehemently denied.

7. C – The barge used to house asylum seekers was called *Bibby Stockholm*. Human rights issues on the barge were constantly under the spotlight, due to the non-zero chance that residents could bump into Suella Braverman.

8. B – Eight people became trapped in a cable car after one of the cables snapped, leaving them dangling nine hundred feet over a river. They were all eventually rescued, and an eight-part Netflix documentary was released fifteen minutes after the last child's feet touched the ground.

9. C – A Lego set released in September utilises the studs on top of the bricks to teach blind and partially sighted children how to read Braille. As an added bonus, they're equally as painful to step on as regular Lego bricks, so they also act as an early warning system for when parents are nearby.

10. A – Two passengers were treated for minor injuries when a tuk-tuk driven by Chris Evans overturned on a racetrack in Hampshire. Spare a thought too for the person who had to call an ambulance and convince them it wasn't a prank call.

TRUE OR FALSE – ROUND 4

One final round of outrageous stories from 2023, but which ones actually happened, and which are fake news?

1. In August, US-based toy maker Mattel conducted a nationwide search for a 'Chief Uno player' offering a weekly salary of more than $4,000.

2. In September, a hotel in Stockport used to house migrants was temporarily closed after occupants claimed it was haunted.

3. In June, a man in Durham was jailed for fourteen days for fly-tipping after throwing a jar of pickled gherkins from his car on the A1.

4. In July the press watchdog ruled that it is not inaccurate to describe Matt Hancock as a 'failed health secretary and cheating husband who broke the lockdown rules he wrote'.

5. In October, a Brazilian hot-air balloon show was condemned by the Vatican after a photograph surfaced of a balloon shaped like the Pope with gigantic breasts.

6. In April, a 'first-edition' copy of the Bible – supposedly signed by Jesus – sold for nearly $6,000 on eBay. Unsurprisingly, it was later confirmed to be a forgery.

7. No fewer than seventeen sets of twins started at schools in the Scottish authority of Inverclyde in September, earning it the nickname 'Twinverclyde'.

8. In October, Channel 4 pulled a Halloween episode of *Gogglebox* from its streaming service after one of its 'stars' dressed up as Jimmy Savile, resulting in more than two hundred complaints.

9. In August, an AI supermarket app in New Zealand began recommending recipes for chlorine gas, poison sandwiches and mosquito-repellent roast potatoes.

10. During Rishi Sunak's summer holiday in California, a fitness TikToker claimed that he joined her Taylor Swift-themed fitness class. Downing Street didn't confirm the news, but did go on record to say that Sunak is a 'Swiftie'.

11. In August, Zoom ordered staff back to the office, despite its business relying heavily on people working from home.

12. In January, archaeologists in Cyprus were stumped when they uncovered a two-thousand-year-old mosaic which appeared to depict a man flying a helicopter.

13. In March, Belfast's *Titanic* museum discovered that a piece of the hull – long thought to be from the famous wreck – was actually from a 1980s fishing trawler.

14. The winner of the 2023 24 Hours of Le Mans race stopped on the finishing straight and crossed the line in reverse, such was his massive lead over the car in second place.

15. Chloe Kelly's winning penalty in England's victory over Nigeria in the World Cup round of sixteen was measured travelling at 110.79km/h – faster than any shot by a man in the 2022–23 Premier League season.

16. In July, California was terrorised by an aggressive group of sea otters that scared surfers and commandeered their surfboards.

17. In April, British boxer Daniel Dubois agreed to fight a kangaroo while on holiday in Australia but pulled out after complaints from animal rights charities.

18. During a summer trip to China, US Treasury Secretary Janet Yellen was alleged to have accidentally consumed magic mushrooms after footage showed her repeatedly bowing to her Chinese counterpart.

19. In September, a seven-year-old boy from Darlington received thirty-one speeding fines after Lithuanian criminals stole his identity.

20. During the 2023 Tour de France, a fan trying to take a selfie caused a twenty-bike pile-up.

TRUE OR FALSE – ROUND 4 ANSWERS

True

1. In August, US-based toy maker Mattel conducted a nationwide search for a 'Chief Uno player' offering a weekly salary of more than $4,000.

4. In July the press watchdog ruled that it is not inaccurate to describe Matt Hancock as a 'failed health secretary and cheating husband who broke the lockdown rules he wrote'.

7. No fewer than seventeen sets of twins started at schools in the Scottish authority of Inverclyde in September, earning it the nickname 'Twinverclyde'.

9. In August, an AI supermarket app in New Zealand began recommending recipes for chlorine gas, poison sandwiches and mosquito-repellent roast potatoes.

10. During Rishi Sunak's summer holiday in California, a fitness TikToker claimed that he joined her Taylor Swift-themed fitness class. Downing Street didn't confirm the news, but did go on record to say that Sunak is a 'Swiftie'.

11. In August, Zoom ordered staff back to the office, despite its business relying heavily on people working from home.

15. Chloe Kelly's winning penalty in England's victory over Nigeria in the World Cup round of sixteen was measured travelling at 110.79km/h – faster than any shot by a man in the 2022–2023 Premier League season.

16. In July, California was terrified by an aggressive group of sea otters that scared surfers and commandeered their surfboards.

18. During a summer trip to China, US Treasury Secretary Janet Yellen was alleged to have accidentally consumed magic mushrooms after footage showed her repeatedly bowing to her Chinese counterpart.

20. During the 2023 Tour de France, a fan trying to take a selfie caused a twenty-bike pile-up.

False

2. A hotel in Stockport used to house migrants wasn't temporarily closed after occupants claimed it was haunted.

3. A man in Durham wasn't jailed for fourteen days for fly-tipping after throwing a jar of pickled gherkins from his car on the A1.

5. The Vatican didn't condemn a Brazilian hot-air balloon show over a balloon shaped like the Pope with gigantic breasts.

6. A 'first-edition' copy of the Bible – supposedly signed by Jesus – did not sell on eBay for nearly $6,000.

8. An episode of *Gogglebox* wasn't pulled from Channel 4 due to a complaint about a Jimmy Savile costume.

12. Archaeologists didn't uncover a helicopter mosaic in Cyprus.

13. Belfast's *Titanic* museum didn't display part of a fishing trawler, thinking it was from the wreck of the Titanic.

14. The winner of the 2023 24 Hours of Le Mans race didn't stop on the finishing straight and cross the line in reverse.

17. British boxer Daniel Dubois didn't agree to fight a kangaroo while on holiday in Australia.

19. A seven-year-old boy from Darlington didn't receive thirty-one speeding fines as a result of identity theft.

HELP DONALD TRUMP REACH THE MEXICAN BORDER

Donald Trump's legal woes stacked up substantially in 2023. Can you help him escape to the Mexican border before they build a wall to keep him out?

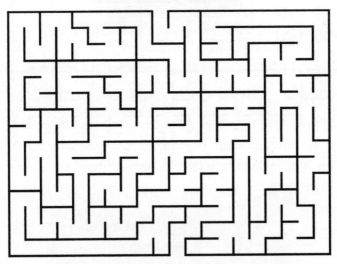

Help Donald Trump Reach the Mexican Border – Solution

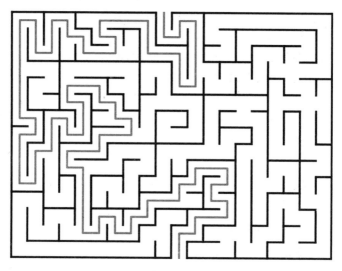

BEFORE OR AFTER THE BIRTH OF BORIS'S BABY BARONESS?

On 12 July Charlotte Owen became the youngest life peer in British history after being nominated by Boris Johnson. One can only conclude that the young blonde woman must have provided exceptionally special advice indeed, as she took her seat in the House of Lords after a career of just eighteen months as his special adviser. Baroness Owen of Alderley Edge was born on 10 May 1993. Did the following things occur before, or after that date?

1. UK release of the Sony PlayStation
2. Dissolution of the Soviet Union
3. O.J. Simpson is acquitted of the murders of Nicole Brown Simpson and Ronald Goldman
4. Nelson Mandela's release from prison
5. John Major becomes PM
6. The launch of the English Premier League
7. Official opening of the Channel Tunnel
8. Queen Elizabeth II's ruby jubilee
9. Margaret Thatcher enters the House of Lords as Baroness Thatcher of Kesteven
10. Rumbelows announces it's closing its doors for the final time

BEFORE OR AFTER THE BIRTH OF BORIS'S BABY BARONESS? – ANSWERS

Before the birth of Boris's baby baroness

2. Dissolution of the Soviet Union (26 December 1991)

4. Nelson Mandela's release from prison (11 February 1990)

5. John Major becomes PM (28 November 1990)

6. The launch of the English Premier League (15 August 1992)

8. Queen Elizabeth II's ruby jubilee (6 February 1992)

9. Margaret Thatcher enters the House of Lords as Baroness Thatcher of Kesteven (30 June 1992)

After the birth of Boris's baby baroness

1. UK release of the Sony PlayStation (29 September 1995)

3. O. J. Simpson is acquitted of the murders of Nicole Brown Simpson and Ronald Goldman (3 October 1995)

7. Official opening of the Channel Tunnel (6 May 1994)

10. Rumbelows announces it's closing its doors for the final time (7 February 1995)

At the seventh annual staging of *Labour's Got Talent*, mind reader Keir the Magnificent was eliminated in the first round after failing to make a single correct prediction:

THE TRUTH IS OUT THERE (APPARENTLY)

On 26 July a former intelligence official testified in a congressional hearing that the United States is in possession of UFOs and 'biologics' of whatever was piloting them. Below are six photos of famous aliens, but – as is often the case with 'evidence' of alien life – they're incredibly blurry. Can you work out who/what they are?

1.   2.

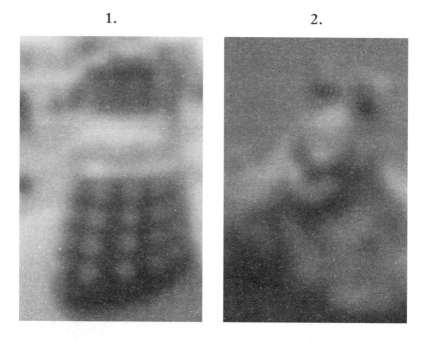

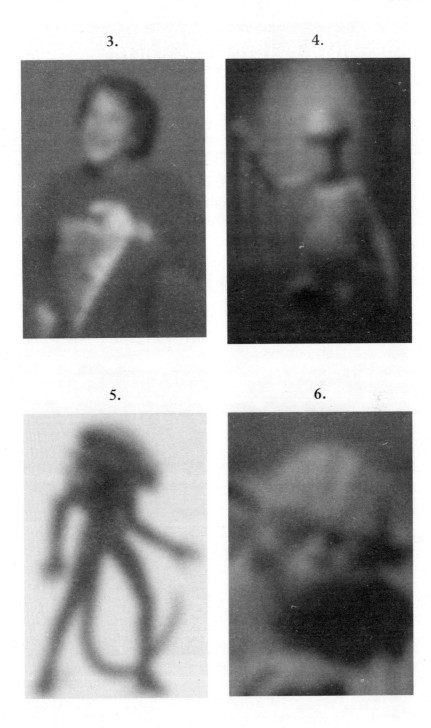

3.

4.

5.

6.

The Truth is Out There (Apparently) – Answers

1. Dalek

2. ALF

3. Mork

4. E.T. the Extra-Terrestrial

5. Xenomorph

6. Yoda

FEEL OLD YET?

The answers to the following questions are all people or things that celebrated major milestones in 2023. Can you put the realisation that we're all marching (some quicker than others) towards the grave to the back of your mind and work them out from the answers below?

1. Steven Spielberg-directed film about an ambitious (and terribly mismanaged) theme park, released thirty years ago, in 1993. In the years since, it has spawned five sequels, all of which have been absolutely terrible.

2. Second album from former boyband member (or if you ask Noel Gallagher, a 'fat dancer'), which turned twenty-five in October. Includes the songs 'No Regrets', 'Millennium' and 'She's the One'.

3. Hollywood actor who celebrated his eightieth birthday in 2023. Credits include *Caddyshack* and *Three Amigos!*, but he is perhaps best known for playing the bumbling Clark Griswold in the National Lampoon films.

4. First published twenty years ago in 2003, this bestselling novel follows the exploits of symbologist Robert Langdon as he runs around Paris solving puzzles while people try to murder him for doing so.

5. Global mega corporation founded by brothers Roy and Walter one hundred years ago, in October 1923.

6. Film following the rise of Tony Montana from penniless immigrant to drug kingpin that celebrated its fortieth anniversary in 2023. Probably a favourite of Michael Gove.

7. BBC show that celebrated its sixtieth anniversary in 2023. Its first episode originally aired on 23 November 1963, but was repeated the following week due to John F. Kennedy selfishly skewing the viewing figures by being assassinated.

8. Eighth studio album from Pink Floyd, released fifty years ago. Tracks include 'Time', 'Money', 'The Great Gig in the Sky' and 'Us and Them'. A famous urban legend states that it was written to sync up perfectly with *The Wizard of Oz*.

9. English actor known for his strong cockney accent. Star of films including *The Dark Knight, Inception* and *The Muppet Christmas Carol*. Celebrated his ninetieth birthday on 14 March.

10. In 1993 Meat Loaf spent seven weeks at number one in the UK Singles Chart with this song. The album version clocks in at just over twelve minutes, although thankfully the radio edit was much (much) shorter.

FEEL OLD YET? – ANSWERS

1. *Jurassic Park*

2. *I've Been Expecting You* – Robbie Williams

3. Chevy Chase

4. *The Da Vinci Code*

5. The Walt Disney Company

6. *Scarface*

7. *Doctor Who*

8. *The Dark Side of the Moon*

9. Michael Caine

10. 'I'd Do Anything for Love (But I Won't Do That)'

MISSING WORDS – ROUND 4

More headlines, bits missing etc. Have at it.

1. Man tries to fool police into thinking he's ＿＿＿＿＿＿
   with driving licence
   Mirror – 2 May

   A. Boris Johnson

   B. Luke Skywalker

   C. Jesus Christ

   D. George Clooney

2. Former royal butler Paul Burrell tells *I'm a Celebrity*
   campmates about the late Queen's ＿＿＿＿＿＿＿
   Mail Online – 27 April

   A. Secret stamp collection

   B. Biggest fear

   C. Bath time routine

   D. Dislike for Danny Dyer

3. Brooklyn Beckham roasted for _____
    with blow torch
    Independent – 26 April

    A. Burning wasp nest
    B. Posing nude
    C. Fixing washing machine
    D. Grilling cheese toastie

4. 'That was a mistake': Steven Spielberg admits he regrets
    removing _____ from *E.T.*
    Screen Rant – 26 April

    A. Nude scene
    B. Drug references
    C. F word
    D. Guns

5. Man in '_____' jumps in front of woman's
    car in Bleadon
    BBC – 9 May

    A. Medieval suit of armour
    B. Clown costume
    C. Gimp suit
    D. See-through body stocking

6. Macron blasted for 'toxic masculinity' after

_____

Express – 20 June

    A. Judging French beauty pageant

    B. Lighting match on his stubble

    C. Saying men shouldn't cry

    D. Downing bottle of beer in 17 seconds

7. Man jailed for performing sex act while

_____

Sky News – 21 June

    A. Kneeling over captured seagull

    B. Riding unicycle through Basildon town centre

    C. Operating the Waltzer on Brighton Pier

    D. Driving past speed cameras on the A690

8. Sunak says he would let robots _____

_____

Independent – 7 June

    A. Advise on key policy decisions

    B. Fill out his tax returns

    C. Look after his grandmother and teach his children

    D. Perform minor surgery, but only under human supervision

9. Man walks six miles to bring his _____ to
   Glastonbury Festival – but says it's 'worth it'
   Wales Online – 23 June

   A. Dining room table
   B. Seven-piece drum kit
   C. Entire double bed
   D. Ninety-year-old grandmother

10. The Perseverance Rover has _____
    Universe Today – 20 April

    A. Lost its pet rock
    B. Started swearing, and nobody knows why
    C. Developed a dirt moustache
    D. Become wedged between two rocks

MISSING WORDS – ROUND 4 ANSWERS

1. A – Man tries to fool police into thinking he's **Boris Johnson** with driving licence. A motorist in the Netherlands who was pulled over and arrested on suspicion of drink driving in May produced a novelty Boris Johnson driving licence. Police say they immediately had suspicions that it wasn't actually Boris Johnson though, as at no point did the car attempt a U-turn.

2. C – Former royal butler Paul Burrell tells *I'm a Celebrity* campmates about the late Queen's **bath time routine**. Paul Burrell has built a successful career based solely on having a job in the 1980s, and in 2023 he revealed details about the Queen's bath-time habits, including bombshells such as how she liked her towels to be set out, and that she didn't like to touch the plug. His *I'm a Celeb* campmate Janice Dickinson said Burrell 'has the best stories on earth', suggesting he's the only person she's ever met.

3. D – Brooklyn Beckham roasted for **grilling cheese toastie** with blow torch. Influencer Brooklyn Beckham – whose talents range from having a famous parent, to having another famous parent – took to Instagram and used a blow torch to ... sorry, it's impossible to write something interesting about Brooklyn Beckham. You're probably not even reading this. On to the next answer ...

4. D – 'That was a mistake': Steven Spielberg admits he regrets removing **guns** from *E.T.* The decision to edit guns out of *E.T.* also changed the famous joke 'what's E.T. short

for?', as the original punchline was 'because his legs were blown off by an AK-47'.

5. C – Man in 'gimp suit' jumps in front of woman's car in Bleadon. The gimp sighting took place in the constituency of Liam Fox, who must have been relieved when police arrested local man Joshua Hunt.

6. D – Macron blasted for 'toxic masculinity' after **downing bottle of beer in 17 seconds**. The French president necked the beer in a rugby dressing room after Toulouse beat La Rochelle in June. In his defence, he spent much of 2023 failing to prevent rioting, so you can understand his excitement at seeing a glass bottle without a flaming rag sticking out of the top.

7. A – Man jailed for performing sex act while **kneeling over captured seagull**. Spare a thought for the seagull, who couldn't believe his luck when he swooped in for what looked like an eight-inch chip.

8. C – Sunak says he would let robots **look after his grandmother and teach his children**. Rishi Sunak made the comments after speaking to Joe Biden about advances in AI technology, which must have felt like talking to a house plant about quantum physics.

9. C – Man walks six miles to bring his **entire double bed** to Glastonbury Festival – but says it's 'worth it'. Constructing the bed required five trips between the campsite and his car, and a fourteen-hour round trip to Edinburgh because he forgot the Allen key.

10. A – The Perseverance Rover has **lost its pet rock**. A 'pet' rock which had been wedged in the Perseverance Rover's wheel arch for more than a year went missing in April, and the chances of getting it back are slim as Mars doesn't have any lamp posts.

After finding himself with a bit of free time following his resignation in April, Dominic Raab immediately ran into problems during a leisurely drive to France:

A Spouse Divided

In March, ninety-two-year-old Rupert Murdoch announced that he was getting married for the fifth time,* saying that it had 'better be' his last (a sentiment shared by most people, although probably not for the same reason). Can you identify the following serial marriers from their long lists of spouses?

1. Conrad Hilton Jr. (m. 1950–div. 1951), Michael Wilding (m. 1952–div. 1957), Mike Todd (m. 1957–d. 1958), Eddie Fisher (m. 1959–div. 1964), Richard Burton (m. 1964–div. 1974), Richard Burton (m. 1975–div. 1976), John Warner (m. 1976–div. 1982), Larry Fortensky (m. 1991–div. 1996)

2. Ivana Zelníčková (m. 1977–div. 1990), Marla Maples (m. 1993–div. 1999), Melania Knauss (m. 2005)

3. Edward C. Judson (m. 1937–d. 1942), Orson Welles (m. 1943–div. 1947), Prince Aly Khan (m. 1949–div. 1953), Dick Haymes (m. 1953–div. 1955), James Hill (m. 1958–div. 1961)

---

* The engagement was called off a few weeks later, so he's either back on the market or the nation is mourning a titan of the media.

4. Melissa Lee Gatlin (m. 1978–div. 1980), Toni Lawrence (m. 1986–div. 1988), Cynda Williams (m. 1990–div. 1992), Pietra Dawn Cherniak (m. 1993–div. 2003), Angelina Jolie (m. 2000–div. 2003), Connie Angland (m. 2014)

5. Peter Andre (m. 2005–div. 2009), Alex Reid (m. 2010–div. 2011), Kieran Hayler (m. 2013–div. 2021)

6. Linda Eastman (m. 1969–d. 1998), Heather Mills (m. 2002–div. 2008), Nancy Shevell (m. 2011)

7. Ojani Noa (m. 1997–div. 1998), Cris Judd (m. 2001–div. 2003), Marc Anthony (m. 2004–div. 2014), Ben Affleck (m. 2022)

8. Patricia Arquette (m. 1995–div. 2001), Lisa Marie Presley (m. 2002–div. 2004), Alice Kim (m. 2004–div. 2016), Erika Koike (m. 2019–div. 2019), Riko Shibata (m. 2021)

9. Tommy Lee (m. 1995–div. 1998), Kid Rock (m. 2006–div. 2007), Rick Salomon (m. 2007–ann. 2008), Rick Salomon (m. 2014–div. 2015), Jon Peters (m. 2020–ann. 2020), Dan Hayhurst (m. 2020–div. 2022)

10. Alana Collins (m. 1979–div. 1984), Rachel Hunter (m. 1990–div. 2006), Penny Lancaster (m. 2007)

A Spouse Divided – Answers

1. Elizabeth Taylor

2. Donald Trump

3. Rita Hayworth

4. Billy Bob Thornton

5. Katie Price

6. Paul McCartney

7. Jennifer Lopez

8. Nicolas Cage

9. Pamela Anderson

10. Rod Stewart

MATCH THE NEPO BABY TO THEIR FAMOUS PARENT

Each year an irritating new phrase becomes popular, and in 2023 it was the turn of 'nepo baby' – that is, celebrities who struggled against the handicap of having a famous parent to give them a leg-up. Can you match the following celebs to the reason for their success?

1.	Angelina Jolie	A.	Goldie Hawn
2.	Maya Hawke	B.	Meg Ryan
3.	Kate Hudson	C.	Denise Welch
4.	Emilio Estevez	D.	Judy Garland
5.	Dakota Johnson	E.	Uma Thurman
6.	Jack Quaid	F.	Melanie Griffith
7.	Liza Minnelli	G.	Steven Spielberg
8.	Riley Keough	H.	Jon Voigt
9.	Jessica Capshaw	I.	Lisa Marie Presley
10.	Matty Healy	J.	Martin Sheen

Match the Nepo Baby to Their Famous Parent – Answers

1. H. Angelina Jolie – Jon Voigt

2. E. Maya Hawke – Uma Thurman

3. A. Kate Hudson – Goldie Hawn

4. J. Emilio Estevez – Martin Sheen

5. F. Dakota Johnson – Melanie Griffith

6. B. Jack Quaid – Meg Ryan

7. D. Liza Minnelli – Judy Garland

8. I. Riley Keough – Lisa Marie Presley

9. G. Jessica Capshaw – Steven Spielberg

10. C. Matty Healy – Denise Welch

Cancel culture strikes again: Gromit and Shaun the Sheep found themselves looking for work after Wallace was pictured at a far-right rally in Dorset:

THE WORLD'S DULLEST CROSSWORD

What could be more fun than a quick crossword? Well not so fast, because this one is all about the Labour Party.

Across

3. John _____, deputy leader of the Labour Party from 1994 to 2007; not a big fan of eggs (8)

6. *Basic* _____, film that Angela Rayner was accused of channelling to distract Boris Johnson in early 2022 (8)

7. Sandwich filling made famous by Ed Miliband in 2014 (5)

11. Emily _____, MP for Islington South and Finsbury since 2005. Has held numerous shadow cabinet positions (10)

Down

1. ___ Livingstone, former mayor of London who was suspended from the Labour Party in 2016 (3)

2. North London constituency held by Diane Abbott since 1987 (7)

4. James _____, prime minister from 1976 to 1979 (9)

5. North African country where Jeremy Corbyn controversially laid a wreath in 2014 (7)

8. First name of Tony Blair's wife (6)

9. Keir Starmer's Peckham-inspired middle name (6)

10. Left-wing grassroots group formed when Jeremy Corbyn become Labour leader in 2015 (8)

THE WORLD'S DULLEST CROSSWORD — ANSWERS

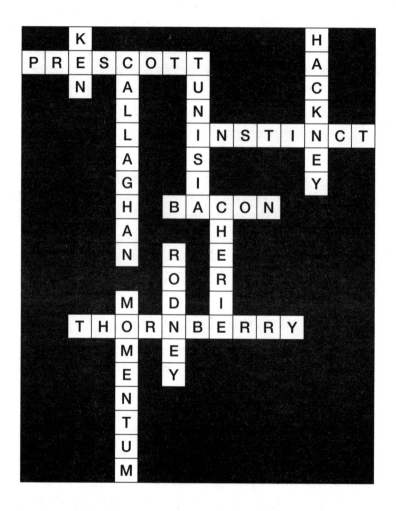

HAPPY(ISH) ENDINGS

In May, the World Health Organization declared that Covid-19 is no longer a 'global health emergency'. Some would dispute this (and indeed, your dad's mate on Facebook is adamant that it's a hoax and never even started). Below are ten occasions from throughout history when other things 'ended'. Can you arrange them into chronological order?

1. The World Health Organization declares smallpox eradicated – the only infectious disease to achieve this distinction

2. Conscription – reintroduced at the start of the Second World War – ends in the UK

3. Authorities declare that the Great Fire of London has been extinguished

4. Genghis Khan dies

5. The Beatles break up, one month before the release of their final album

6. Michelangelo finishes painting the Sistine Chapel

7. British military involvement in Afghanistan ends after the final troops touch down at RAF Brize Norton

8. The fall of the Roman Empire

9. Music sharing website Napster ceases operations after losing multiple lawsuits

10. The final episode of *Only Fools and Horses* airs in the UK

Happy(ish) Endings – Answers

1. The fall of the Roman Empire (AD 476)

2. Genghis Khan dies (1227)

3. Michelangelo finishes painting the Sistine Chapel (1512)

4. Authorities declare that the Great Fire of London has been extinguished (1666)

5. Conscription – reintroduced at the start of the Second World War – ends in the UK (1960)

6. The Beatles break up, one month before the release of their final album (1970)

7. The World Health Organization declares smallpox eradicated – the only infectious disease to achieve this distinction (1980)

8. Music sharing website Napster ceases operations after losing multiple lawsuits (2001)

9. The final episode of *Only Fools and Horses* airs in the UK (2003)

10. British military involvement in Afghanistan ends after the final troops touch down at RAF Brize Norton (2021)

Bonus question from Have I Got News for You: The Quiz of 2022

The elephantine-memory-endowed among you will remember that in last year's book, we asked you a bonus question:

How many words does this book contain?

Well, you'll be pleased to know that the answer is: 46,689

BONUS QUESTION (WHICH IS IN NO WAY A PLOY TO PLUG THE NEXT BOOK)

How many times did the word 'news' appear in this book?

Bonus question – answer

Find out in the next instalment of the *Have I Got News for You* quiz book!

Picture Credits

1991

To:
    Alyson.

Happy 7th Birthday

Love:
    Lesley. Gary. Simon and Amy
      x   x   x   x